高校英语选修课系列教材

Selected Readings of English Dramas

英语戏剧读本选编

主编：李成坚
编者：张志佑 郑博仁 闫　静

清华大学出版社
北　京

内容简介

本书共收入11位著名剧作家的11篇戏剧选段。全书按照剧作家和作品选段共分为11个单元。每个单元均包含5大板块：剧作家简介、剧情介绍、名篇选读、拓展思考、延展阅读。这5大板块的有机结合既有利于教师系统讲解，同时也方便学生自学。

本书适合广大高校开设英美文学课程的授课教师、英语专业学生、非英语专业对英美文学感兴趣的学生及欲提高英美文学素养的读者使用。

图书在版编目（CIP）数据

英语戏剧读本选编 / 李成坚主编；张志佑，郑博仁，闫静编.
北京：清华大学出版社，2016（2024.8重印）
高校英语选修课系列教材
ISBN 978-7-302-44339-1

Ⅰ.①英… Ⅱ.①李… ②张… ③郑… ④闫… Ⅲ.①英语-阅读教学-高等学校-教材 ②戏剧文学-剧本-作品集-世界 Ⅳ.①H319.4：I

中国版本图书馆CIP数据核字（2016）第163027号

责任编辑：徐博文
封面设计：平　原
责任校对：王凤芝
责任印制：刘　菲
出版发行：清华大学出版社

网　　址：https://www.tup.com.cn，https://www.wqxuetang.com
地　　址：北京清华大学学研大厦A座　　邮　　编：100084
社 总 机：010-83470000　　邮　　购：010-62786544
投稿与读者服务：010-62776969, c-service@tup.tsinghua.edu.cn
质量反馈：010-62772015, zhiliang@tup.tsinghua.edu.cn

印 装 者：三河市人民印务有限公司
经　　销：全国新华书店
开　　本：185mm×260mm　　**印　　张**：12.75　　**字　　数**：246千字
版　　次：2016年7月第1版　　**印　　次**：2024年8月第2次印刷
定　　价：59.00元

产品编号：067866-02

前言
Forewords

戏剧作为文学创作的形式之一，有着悠远的历史。尽管戏剧的起源至今并无最终的定论，诸多戏剧理论都认同两种基本的假设。第一种，戏剧源自于仪式演化。人类在尚无力理解、解释和抗衡自然力量时，通过群体性的仪式（祭祀、典礼等）活动，表达对自然神秘力量的敬畏和祈求，对神和英雄人物的歌颂和赞美，以获得某种希冀中的拯救力量。第二种，戏剧起源于庆祝丰收时的即兴歌舞表演，源自于酒神祭祀。巫师戴上神或鬼的面具，成为神鬼的代言人。因此，戏剧是与歌舞紧密相连的一种古老的艺术表现形式之一。

与诗歌和小说这两种文类相比，戏剧的独特性在于它是一种舞台表演艺术。这种舞台表演艺术集合了语言、动作、舞蹈、音乐等形式，以达到叙述目的。就表演形式而言，戏剧包括话剧、歌剧、舞剧、音乐剧等。文学上戏剧的概念其实是指为戏剧表演所创作的脚本，即剧本。作为相较于诗歌和小说更为大众化和娱乐化的艺术形式，戏剧最终的艺术呈现是舞台呈现（performance on stage）而非剧本本身（play on page）。与中国戏剧一样，观众在赏析西方戏剧时，不能仅止于对剧本的研读，更多的是要去感受舞台上戏剧的艺术呈现，并从根本上研究戏剧的其他三个要素：演员、观众、剧场。

戏剧具有六要素：形象、性格、情节、言辞、歌曲和思想，其中情节最为重要。西方戏剧诞生于2400多年前的古希腊时期。就剧种而言，有悲剧和喜剧两种。悲剧起源于酒神赞美歌的序曲；喜剧起源于下等表演的序曲，其原意是“狂欢游行之歌”。公元前5世纪，亚里士多德就在其理论论著《诗学》中界定了悲剧与喜剧的差异：悲剧是对英雄的赞美，而喜剧则是对小人滑稽的嘲笑，因为他们存在性格和行为的心理缺陷。亚氏的《诗学》中有大量篇幅探讨戏剧，尤其是悲剧的创作与特征。悲剧是严肃的、完整的、对一定长度的行为的模仿；喜剧是对事件和人物的模仿。观众观看悲剧时会产生怜悯与恐惧，最终实现宣泄和净化的目的。

古希腊时期诞生了三位重要的悲剧作家和他们的扛鼎之作：埃斯库罗斯的《被缚的普罗米修斯》强调神性之悲（真理与自我之间的选择）；索福克勒斯的《俄狄浦斯王》突出命运之悲；欧里庇得斯的《美狄亚》凸显人性之思。这三大悲剧都是世界经典戏剧，并被后世剧作家不断地借用创作。

近代，以莎士比亚为代表的戏剧创作无疑是16世纪欧洲文艺复兴时期戏剧繁荣的典型代表。莎士比亚汲取中世纪宗教和民间文化，勾勒出一个发展强大、雄心壮志的英国王朝及其这一时代背景下的英雄群像。在艺术形式上，莎士比亚打破锁闭式结构，强调悲剧美感，将悲喜剧杂糅。他的人物刻画展现了多面的人性，呈现了生动而复杂的时代特征。莎士比亚不仅铸就了伊丽莎白女王时代的戏剧辉煌，更超越了这一时代，成为永恒的、世界性的莎翁。

17世纪，以法国为代表的古典主义戏剧强调创作的规范，提出“三一律（Three unities of time, place and action）”，要求戏剧所叙述的故事发生在一天之内，地点在一个场景，情节服从于一个主题。在形式上，“三一律”严格区分悲剧和喜剧，强调二者之间的严格界限。以高乃依和拉辛为代表的悲剧强调“逼真”“典雅”“理性”，体现尊重王权、尊重理性的时代特征；而以莫里哀为代表的喜剧则强调反教会、反封建的意识，更具民间性、娱乐性特色。

英国对古典主义戏剧的接受是在王朝复辟（1660年）之后，以德莱顿为代表。尽管德莱顿的戏剧作品到今天已少有人问津，但其卓绝敏睿的文学趣味使他作为英国第一文人突破了当时古典主义的审美框架，发掘和称颂莎士比亚戏剧的独到和魅力，开创了18世纪英国新古典主义戏剧时代。新古典主义打破“三一律”的法规，打破悲剧和喜剧的严格划分，开始采用正剧体裁。在语体形式上，戏剧对话使用散文形式，而不再是诗体或韵文（16—17世纪盛行的诗剧），将辛辣的讽刺和严密的说理相结合，充分体现了“理性”的时代特征。

18世纪下半叶，浪漫主义戏剧兴起。浪漫主义戏剧主要集中在德、法两国，以雨果、大仲马等剧作家为代表，力图突破古典主义的原则，崇尚主观，强调艺术家的想象、激情与灵感。浪漫主义戏剧意图摆脱艺术程式的束缚，其艺术的反抗性和力量更多地体现在诗歌和小说之中。在英国，浪漫主义诗人拜伦和雪莱在创作诗歌之余，兼顾戏剧形式，如拜伦的《曼弗雷德》《该隐》和雪莱的《解放了的普罗米修斯》，这些都是诗剧。

19世纪现实主义戏剧抬头，诞生了一大批重要的剧作家，如挪威的易卜生、俄国的契诃夫、英国的萧伯纳。在艺术表现方面，现实主义戏剧将客观真实地再现生活作为基本准则。他们主张在舞台上严格地按照生活的逻辑组织冲突和场面。无论对人物的心理刻画，还是对动作细节的描绘，现实主义戏剧都尽可能做到逼真和准确。剧作家不能像浪漫主义戏剧那样，借人物之口直接抒发自己的情感和议论，而必须通过客观的舞台形象自然地流露作者的社会理想和道德激情。为使舞台形象真实可信，现实主义戏剧的结构通常具有时间、地点和事件比较集中紧凑的特点。台词采用生活化的语言。与此同时，现实主义戏剧又强调艺术的典型化原则，反对把生活现象不加选择地搬上舞台的自然主义倾向。他们要求戏剧通过典型的环境、事件（情节）和冲突，来烘托、突出典型性格，从而深刻地揭示社会生活的某些本质方面及其发展趋势。

进入20世纪，西方文学也进入了现代主义时期。现代主义是一个十分宽泛的概念，泛指包括文学、绘画、雕塑、音乐等艺术形式在内的艺术创作流派。现代主义以一种前所未有的大胆，变革以往以现实主义为基调的创作原则和范式，以变形、夸张、离奇的手法和形式展现20世纪的人们对世界的认知和感受。在戏剧方面，以奥尼尔、田纳西、米勒等为代表的剧作家运用大量内心独白、幻象和梦境等形式展现人内在的本质，是为表现主义戏剧；以贝克特等为代表的荒诞派戏剧则摈弃传统的语言、结构和情节上的逻辑和连贯性，以松散的情节结构、充满喜剧的舞台效果隐喻悲剧的内在，展现世界的荒诞本质。

戏剧的发展历程无疑是与整个西方文学的发展史一脉相承的。戏剧作为一种有别于诗歌和小说的文类形式，有其自身的艺术突破和创新的内在驱动，即包括语言、情节、结构、舞台等方面的不断变化与改革，正是这一艺术突破的内在要求，使得戏剧艺术及其舞台魅力绵延至今。

纵观国内现行的戏剧教材读本，数量不多，但质量精良。例如，何其莘主编的《英国戏剧选读》和傅俊主编的《英国戏剧读本》（上、下）强调国别文学特征和断代文学特征；刘海平等主编的《英美戏剧：作品与评论》强调以戏剧要素为核心的文学指导，具有很强的学术性；陈红薇、王岚主编的《二十世纪英国戏剧》以第二次世界大战为时间轴线，对战前和战后的戏剧文学进行了全面的概述，并将爱尔兰岛的爱尔兰文艺复兴、新戏剧和女性声音展现了全貌。

任何一本文学文本选集都是编者审美趣味的体现。要将众多的文学大家和众多的作品在一本教材里最恰当、最充分地体现，遴选本身就是一个考验。选择哪位代表作家，选用作家的哪个文本，利用文本中哪段作为阅读选段无不包含着编者的意图和旨趣。毋庸置疑，这本《英语戏剧读本选编》自然也是编者文学爱好和趣味的彰显。与其他选本不同的是，本教材隐含着一种“爱尔兰视角”。

《英语戏剧读本选编》共入编11位剧作家，这些剧作家都是读者耳熟能详的名字，如莎士比亚、王尔德、萧伯纳、奥尼尔、叶芝、辛格等。从国别来看，本教材涵盖英国（如莎士比亚）、美国（如奥尼尔）和爱尔兰（如叶芝等）；从经典和当代兼顾来看，本教材尽可能呈现英语戏剧发展的历史演进，反映英语世界的戏剧成果。编者在遴选剧本时，节选重要片段，使读者真切地感受英语文本的质感，品味戏剧作品的语言魅力和作家的智性魅力。

相较于以往的戏剧读本教材，本教材的不同之处有两个方面：

第一，入选的11位作家虽独立成篇，但他们都有一个共同点：他们或他们的作品都与爱尔兰有着或隐或显、或深或浅的关联。莎士比亚的历史剧《亨利五世》呈现了爱尔兰人的形象以及英国与爱尔兰之间微妙的民族关系，从这一选段中读者可以窥探莎士比亚戏剧内涵的丰富性以及莎士比亚戏剧所背依时代的复杂性。一直被视为英国作家的王尔德和萧伯纳实则都出身爱尔兰，尽管他们的作品多以伦敦为创作背景，但他们的作品都能反映出他们文化身份中的爱尔兰性征。奥尼尔作为20世纪美国表现主义戏剧的代表人物，是众多爱尔兰裔美国人的后代之一。其戏剧作品同样有着反映其爱尔兰文化背景的痕迹。近年来，从“散居”的视角重读盎格鲁—爱尔兰作家和爱尔兰裔美国作家，发掘他们作品中的爱尔兰意识，成为国内外学术界关注的热点之一。叶芝、辛格、奥卡西等剧作家无疑都是20世纪爱尔兰戏剧民族化的重要推动者。正是由于叶芝及其创建的阿贝剧院（Abbey Theatre）开创了爱尔兰戏剧的新时代，在20世纪下半叶，以弗里尔、卡尔和麦克多纳为代表的剧作家续写和发展了爱尔兰戏剧文学的辉煌。因此，用爱尔兰视角将这11位作家串接起来，使读者透过文学文本线性地把握16世纪到20世纪爱尔兰社会的历程，是本教材编者的意图所在。本教材的文后附录2“走近爱尔兰”简述爱尔兰历史，亦旨在帮助读者更深入地理解。

第二，入选的剧目多是在以前的选本中不曾出现过的。例如，莎士比亚的历史剧《亨利五世》、萧伯纳的《英国佬的另一个岛》、奥尼尔的《诗人的气质》，以及绝大部分为现行的“英美戏剧读本”所忽略的爱尔兰剧作家和他们的作品。如此之目的，一来编者试图拓展国内读者对于西方经典作家的阅读面，扩展他们对于经典作品的认知度；二来编者以为，在国家“一带一路”倡议下，基于国别（区域）的文化研究和经济—文化并行的策略实乃确保国家战略顺利推进的要义。爱尔兰是欧盟区域的重要国家之一，读者了解爱尔兰的历史、文化、民族发展历程是十分必要的。读者在一定程度上可以打破思维中惯常的国别定势认知，并且意识到国族之间的文学关系原来可以如此之紧密关联。以（戏剧）文学和爱尔兰视角为双重线索的切入，从而打破惯有的认知定势是本教材编者的一次探索尝试。

本教材遵循常规体例格式，分为剧作家简介、剧情介绍、名篇选读、拓展思考及延展阅读五个部分。其中，拓展思考可以引导读者有意识地从爱尔兰的角度进行定向思考，延展阅读则力图给读者提供超越本教材选段的拓展延伸阅读的信息。拓展思考和延展阅读也同时旨在凸显本教材的选篇目的和教材特色。

本教材既可以作为英语专业学生的英语戏剧课程之用，也可以面向非英语专业学生，作为大学生人文通识课程教材之用，亦可供广大戏剧文学爱好者阅读和赏析。在教材的使用过程中，我们建议以课堂引导和讨论戏剧文本为主。遴选的11位剧作家可以在11个教学周内展开，每个剧本讨论一周（2学时）。作为戏剧教学课，我们也强烈建议教师指导学生充分利用这些选段或剧本，展开（模拟）舞台演出。戏剧表演既是文本细读的有效方式，又是培养受教者艺术感受力的途径，戏剧教育在西方也一直是实施人格和人文教育的重要手段。因此，戏剧表演也应该成为戏剧教学乃至戏剧教育的重要组成部分。

本教材的编写是我在电子科技大学工作时校研究生院的资助项目。在本项目资助期间，我调动至西南交通大学工作，本教材最终得以脱稿，也得到了双校人员的支持。

教材编写具体分工如下：

李成坚负责教材的整体统筹规划、内容（作家和作品）遴选、体例设计和教材的最后统稿。西南交通大学英语系教师张志佑、郑博仁、闫静参与各章选段的注释和校对工作。电子科技大学和西南交通大学的研究生王喆、王洁琼、李缘、王贞贞、邓运华等参与了教材英文部分的录入工作。在此，我对老师和研究生们的工作表示感谢！

由于本人学识有限，本教材的不足之处在所难免，愿读者批评指正。

主编

2016年5月

于四川·成都

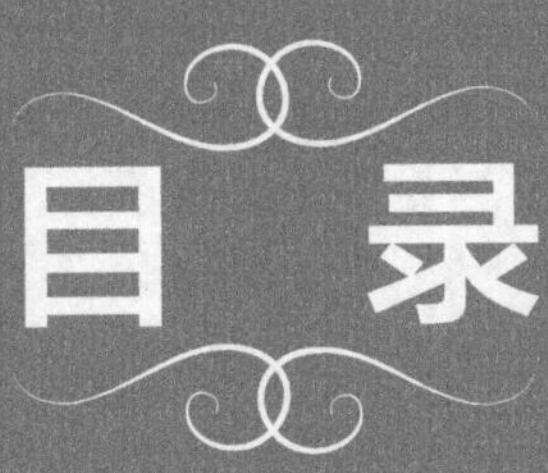

目录

CHAPTER 1

威廉·莎士比亚

William Shakespeare

《亨利五世》

Henry V

一、剧作家简介

威廉·莎士比亚（William Shakespeare，1564—1616）是16世纪英国文艺复兴时期最杰出的剧作家和诗人。他一生创作丰硕，作品包括37部戏剧、154首十四行诗、两首长叙事诗和其他诗歌。他从英国历史和现实中汲取和提炼出广泛的题材，深刻地再现英国文艺复兴时期丰富而复杂的社会生活和精神世界。莎士比亚的创作既属于他所生活的时代，同时又能超越时代的拘囿，为读者提供无限解读的可能。莎士比亚是永恒和经典的，他被喻为“人类文学奥林匹克山上的宙斯”，在世界文学史上享有至高殊荣。

莎士比亚的戏剧大体分为四类：历史剧、喜剧、悲剧和悲喜剧（又称传奇剧）。莎士比亚的四大喜剧《威尼斯商人》（*The Merchant of Venice*）、《仲夏夜之梦》（*A Midsummer Night's Dream*）、《皆大欢喜》（*As You Like It*）、《第十二夜》（*Twelfth Night*）和四大悲剧《哈姆雷特》（*Hamlet*）、《奥赛罗》（*Othello*）、《李尔王》（*King Lear*）、《麦克白》（*Macbeth*）广为人知，也被认为是他戏剧成就的最高代表。他与古希腊三大悲剧家埃斯库罗斯（Aeschylus）、索福克里斯（Sophocles）及欧里庇得斯（Euripides）合称戏剧史上四大悲剧家。

莎士比亚的历史剧通常为读者所忽视。事实上，以11世纪以来英国历史为题材的历史剧是莎士比亚借古喻今的有效途径，这些历史剧记录了英国民族意识崛起之时的雄心斗志和复杂矛盾。历史剧一方面是英国社会主导意识形态的反映；另一方面，通过舞台的表演使主导意识形态实现社会层面的流通，形塑戏剧观众的价值观念。

二、剧情简介

《亨利五世》（*Henry V*）是莎士比亚历史剧“亨利王系列”中的重要剧作，也是历史剧四部曲的终曲。《亨利五世》之前是《理查二世》（*Richard II*，1595）、《亨利四世第一部》（*Henry IV*，*part 1*，1597）和《亨利四世第二部》（*Henry IV*，*part 2*，1599）。

据考证，《亨利五世》创作于1599年。故事聚焦英格兰国王亨利五世，以百年战争期间阿金库尔战役（Battle of Agincourt）为时间轴心。该剧着重突出亨利精心筹备与法国开战的战事布局，机智挫败针对亨利五世的暗杀计划，处决包括剑桥伯爵在内的暗杀者，最后成功迎娶法国公主为妻的整个过程，凸显了亨利五世作为英国一代君王的无比智慧和莫大勇气。

本章节选《亨利五世》中的两个戏剧选段。第一段是第三幕第二场：四个分别来自英格兰、苏格兰、威尔士和爱尔兰的军官之间的对话场景。第二段是全剧的第五幕也是最后一幕的开场，描述英国大胜法国后，大臣胜利返回伦敦时，市民出城迎接的盛景。这两处中对于爱尔兰人麦克莫里斯和征服爱尔兰的“错误”史实的描述非常值得读者玩味，对于爱尔兰人和爱尔兰事物的描写并不占全剧的中心，但正是这些有趣的旁枝细节更有利于读者有效地窥探16世纪下半叶英爱关系及英格兰作家的文化中心主义意识。

三、名篇选读

Henry V

Act Ⅲ　Scene Ⅱ　Before Harfleur[1]

(*Enter Nym, Bardolph, Pistol, and Boy*[2])

BARDOLPH: On, on, on, on, on! to the breach, to the breach!

NYM: Pray thee[3] corporal, stay; the knocks are too hot[4], and for mine own part I have not a case of lives. The humour of it is too hot[5]; that is the very plain-song[6] of it.

PISTOL: The plain-song is most just; for humours do abound[7];
Knocks go and come;
God's vassals drop and die;
And sword and shield,
In bloody field,
Doth[8] win immortal fame.

BOY: Would I were in an alehouse in London! I would give all my fame for a pot of ale and safety.

PISTOL: And I:

If wishes would prevail with me,
My purpose should not fail with me,
But thither would I hie[9].

BOY: As duly, but not as truly,
As bird doth sing on bough.

(*Enter FLUELLEN*)

FLUELLEN: Up to the breach, you dogs! avaunt, you cullions!

(*Driving them forward*)

PISTOL: Be merciful, great duke, to men of mould[10].
Abate thy rage, abate thy manly rage;
Abate thy rage, great duke!
Good bawcock, bate thy rage; use lenity, sweet chuck[11]!

NYM: These be good humours! your honour wins bad humours.

(*Exeunt all but Boy*)

BOY: As young as I am, I have observed these three swashers. I am boy to them all three; but all they three, though they would serve me, could not be man to me; for indeed three such antics do not amount to a man. For Bardolph, he is white-livered and red-faced; by the means whereof a faces it out, but fights not. For Pistol, he hath a killing tongue and a quiet sword[12]; by the means whereof a breaks words, and keeps whole weapons. For Nym, he hath heard that men of few words are the best men, and therefore he scorns to say his prayers lest'a should be thought a coward; but his few bad words are matched with as few good deeds; for'a never broke any man's head but his own, and that was against a post when he was drunk. They will steal anything, and call it purchase. Bardolph stole a lute-case, bore it twelve leagues[13], and sold it for three halfpence. Nym and Bardolph are sworn brothers in filching, and in Calais they stole a fire-shovel; I knew by that piece of service the men would carry coals. They would have me as familiar with men's pockets as their gloves or their handkerchers; which makes much against my manhood, if I should take from another's pocket to put into mine; for it is plain pocketing up of wrongs. I must leave them, and seek some better service; their villainy goes against my weak stomach, and therefore I must cast it up.

(*Exit*)

(*Re-enter FLUELLEN, GOWER following*)

GOWER: Captain Fluellen, you must come presently to the mines; the Duke of Gloucester[14] would speak with you.

FLUELLEN: To the mines! Tell you the duke, it is not so good to come to the mines; for, look you, the mines is not according to the disciplines of the war; the concavities of it is not sufficient; for, look you, th'adversary—you may discuss unto the Duke, look you—is dig himself four yard under the countermines; by Cheshu, I think'a will plow up all, if there is not better directions.

GOWER: The Duke of Gloucester, to whom the order of the siege is given, is altogether directed by an Irishman, a very valiant gentleman, i' faith.

FLUELLEN: It is Captain Macmorris, is it not?

GOWER: I think it be.

FLUELLEN: By Cheshu, he is an ass, as in the world; I will verify as much in his beard; He has no more directions in the true disciplines of the wars, look you, of the Roman disciplines, than is a puppy-dog.

(*Enter MACMORRIS and Captain JAMY*)

GOWER: Here'a comes; and the Scots captain, Captain Jamy, with him.

FLUELLEN: Captain Jamy is a marvellous falorous gentleman, that is certain, and of great expedition and knowledge in th'ancient wars, upon my particular knowledge of his directions. By Cheshu, he will maintain his argument as well as any military man in the world, in the disciplines of the pristine wars of the Romans.

JAMY: I say gud-day, Captain Fluellen.

FLUELLEN: God-den to your worship, good Captain James.

GOWER: How now, Captain Macmorris! Have you quit the mines? Have the pioneers given o'er?

MACMORRIS: By Chrish, la! tish ill done! The work ish give over; the trompet sound the retreat. By my hand, I swear, and my father's soul, the work ish ill done; it ish give over. I would have blowed up the town, so Chrish save me, la! in an hour. O, tish ill done, tish ill done; by my hand, tish ill done[15]!

FLUELLEN: Captain Macmorris, I beseech you now; will you vouchsafe me; look you, a few disputations with you, as partly touching or concerning the disciplines of the war, the Roman wars, in the way of argument; look you, and friendly communication, partly to satisfy my opinion, and partly for the satisfaction; look you, of my mind, as touching the direction of the military discipline; that is the point.

JAMY: It sall be vary gud, gud feith, gud captains bath; and I sall quit you with gud leve, as I may pick occasion; that sall I, marry[16].

MACMORRIS: It is no time to discourse, so Chrish save me. The day is hot, and the weather, and the wars, and the King, and the Dukes; it is no time to discourse. The town is beseeched, and the trumpet call us to the breach; and we talk, and, be Chrish, do nothing. 'Tis shame for us all, so God sa'me. 'tis shame to stand still; it is shame, by my hand; and there is throats to be cut, and works to be done, and there ish nothing done, so Chrish sa'me, la!

JAMY: By the mess, ere theise eyes of mine take themselves to slomber, ay'll de gud service, or I'll lig i'the grund for it; ay, or go to death; and I'll pay't as valorously as I may, that sall I suerly do, that is the breff and the long. Marry, I wad full fain heard some question 'tween you tway[17].

FLUELLEN: Captain Macmorris, I think, look you, under your correction, there is not many of your nation-

MACMORRIS: Of my nation! What ish my nation? Ish a villain, and a bastard, and a knave, and a rascal. What ish my nation? Who talks of my nation?

FLUELLEN: Look you, if you take the matter otherwise than is meant, Captain Macmorris, peradventure I shall think you do not use me with that affability as in discretion you ought to use me; look you, being as good a man as yourself, both in the disciplines of war and in the derivation of my birth, and in other particularities.

MACMORRIS: I do not know you so good a man as myself; so Chrish save me, I will cut off your head.

GOWER: Gentlemen both, you will mistake each other.

JAMY: Ah! That's a foul fault.

(*A parley sounded*)

GOWER: The town sounds a parley.

FLUELLEN: Captain Macmorris, when there is more better opportunity to be required, look you, I will be so bold as to tell you I know the disciplines of war, and there is an end.

(*Exeunt*)

Act V PROLOGUE

(*Enter CHORUS*)

CHORUS: Vouchsafe to those that have not read the story that I may prompt them; and of such as have, I humbly pray them to admit th' excuse of time, of numbers, and due course of things, which cannot in their huge and proper life Be here presented. Now we bear the King Toward Calais. Grant him there. There seen, heave him away upon your winged thoughts athwart the sea. Behold, the English beach Pales in the flood with men, with wives, and boys, whose shouts and claps out-voice the deep-mouth'd sea, which, like a mighty whiffler, fore the King Seems to prepare his way. So let him land, and solemnly see him set on to London. So swift a pace hath thought that even now you may imagine him upon Blackheath[18]; where that his lords desire him to have borne His bruised helmet and his bended sword before him through the city. He forbids it, being free from vainness and self-glorious pride; giving full trophy, signal, and ostent, quite from himself to God. But now behold In the quick forge and working-house of thought, how London doth pour out her citizens! The mayor and all his brethren in best sort—like to the senators of th'antique Rome, with the plebeians swarming at their heels-Go forth and fetch their conqu'ring Caesar in; As, by a lower but loving likelihood, were now the General of our gracious Empress[19]—As in good time he may—from Ireland coming, Bringing rebellion broached on his sword, How many would the peaceful city quit to welcome him! Much more, and much more cause, did they this Harry. Now in London place him. As yet the lamentation of the French invites the King of England's stay at home; The Emperor's coming in behalf of France to order peace between them; and omit All the occurrences, whatever chanc'd, till Harry's back-return again to France. There must we bring him; and myself have play'd The interim, by rememb'ring you 'tis past. Then brook abridgment; and your eyes advance, after your thoughts, straight back again to France.

(*Exit*)

Act V Scene I France The English camp

(*Enter FLUELLEN and GOWER*)

GOWER: Nay, that's right; but why wear you your leek today? Saint Davy's day is past.

FLUELLEN: There is occasions and causes why and wherefore in all things. I will tell you, ass my friend, Captain Gower: the rascally, scald, beggarly, lousy, pragging knave, Pistol, which you and yourself and all the world know to be no petter than a fellow; look you now, of no merits, he is come to me and prings me pread and salt yesterday; look you, and bid me eat my leek; it was in place where I could not breed no contention with him; but I will be so bold as to wear it in my cap till I see him once again, and then I will tell him a little piece of my desires.

(*Enter PISTOL*)

GOWER: Why, here he comes, swelling like a turkey-cock.

FLUELLEN: 'Tis no matter for his swellings nor his turkey-cocks. God bless you, Aunchient Pistol! You scurvy, lousy knave, God bless you!

PISTOL: Ha! art thou bedlam? dost thou thirst, base Troyan, to have me fold up Parca's fatal web? Hence! I am qualmish at the smell of leek.

FLUELLEN: I peseech you heartily, scurvy, lousy knave, at my desires, and my requests, and my petitions, to eat; look you, this leek; because look you, you do not love it, nor your affections and your appetites and

	your digestions does not agree with it, I would desire you to eat it.
PISTOL:	Not for Cadwallader and all his goats.
FLUELLEN:	There is one goat for you. (*Strikes him*) Will you be so good, scald knave, as eat it?
PISTOL:	Base Trojan, thou shalt die.
FLUELLEN:	You say very true, scald knave, when God's will is. I will desire you to live in the mean time, and eat your victuals; come, there is sauce for it. (*Strikes him*) You call'd me yesterday mountain-squire; but I will make you to-day a squire of low degree. I pray you, fall to; if you can mock a leek, you can eat a leek.
GOWER:	Enough, captain; you have astonished him.
FLUELLEN:	I say, I will make him eat some part of my leek, or I will peat his pate four days. Bite, I pray you; it is good for your green wound and your ploody coxcomb.
PISTOL:	Must I bite?
FLUELLEN:	Yes, certainly, and out of doubt and out of question too, and ambiguities.
PISTOL:	By this leek, I will most horribly revenge; I eat and eat, I swear-
FLUELLEN:	Eat, I pray you; will you have some more sauce to your leek? There is not enough leek to swear by.
PISTOL:	Quiet thy cudgel; thou dost see I eat.
FLUELLEN:	Much good do you, scald knave, heartily. Nay, pray you, throw none away; the skin is good for your broken coxcomb. When you take occasions to see leeks hereafter, I pray you, mock at'em; that is all.
PISTOL:	Good.
FLUELLEN:	Ay, leeks is good. Hold you, there is a groat to heal your pate.
PISTOL:	Me a groat!
FLUELLEN:	Yes, verily and in truth, you shall take it; or I have another leek in my pocket, which you shall eat.
PISTOL:	I take thy groat in earnest of revenge.
FLUELLEN:	If I owe you anything, I will pay you in cudgels; you shall be a

woodmonger, and buy nothing of me but cudgels. God b' wi' you, and keep you, and heal your pate.

(*Exit*)

PISTOL: All hell shall stir for this.

GOWER: Go, go; you are a counterfeit cowardly knave. Will you mock at an ancient tradition, begun upon an honourable respect, and worn as a memorable trophy of predeceased valour and dare not avouch in your deeds any of your words? I have seen you gleeking and galling at this gentleman twice or thrice. You thought, because he could not speak English in the native garb, he could not therefore handle an English cudgel; you find it otherwise, and henceforth let a Welsh correction teach you a good English condition. Fare ye well.

(*Exit*)

PISTOL: Doth Fortune play the huswife with me now?
News have I, that my Nell is dead i' the spital
Of malady of France,
And there my rendezvous is quite cut off.
Old I do wax; and from my weary limbs
Honour is cudgell'd. Well, bawd I'll turn,
And something lean to cutpurse of quick hand.
To England will I steal, and there I'll steal.
And patches will I get unto these cudgell'd scars,
And swear I got them in the Gallia[20] wars.

(*Exit*)

注释

1. **Harfleur:** 勒阿弗尔（Le Havre，又名哈佛尔）是法国北部诺曼底地区继里昂之后的第二大城市，位于塞纳河河口，濒临英吉利海峡。

2. **Nym, Bardolph, Pistol, and Boy:** 剧中第二幕出现的人物，前三个人来自市井，是结拜兄弟。在军队里，尼姆（Nym）是武长（corporal），巴道夫（Bardolph）是中尉（lieutenant），毕斯托尔（Pistol）是旗官（ancient），童儿（Boy）是他们三人的侍从。

3. **thee:** 古英语thou（你）的宾格。
4. **knocks:** 字面意思是敲门声，此处指号令；hot的意思是紧迫的。
5. 本句的意思是：号令太紧迫，叫人受不了。
6. **plain-song:** 不唱高调。
7. 本句的意思是：不唱高调倒也好，一唱起来可带劲了。
8. **doth:** 动词do的古英语第三人称单数形式。
9. 本句的意思是：急急忙忙地就往那儿赶。
10. **men of mould:** 凡人。
11. **sweet chuck:** 知心朋友。
12. 此句使用了修辞上的对比法（antithesis）：a killing tongue and a quiet sword 形成对比，讽刺毕斯托尔爱说大话，但贪生怕死。
13. **league:** 里格（长度单位，约等于 3 英里）。
14. **Gloucester:** 格洛斯特，英国英格兰西南部城市、郡治，与威尔斯相邻。
15. 本段台词的意思是：天哪，啊，太糟糕了！工事停了，回营的号已经吹过了。我举手起誓——加上我老爷子的灵魂，工事太糟了！地道已经放弃了。本来在一个钟头内，我就可以把那个城市毁掉——耶稣救我吧！唉，太糟了！太糟了！我举手起誓，太糟了！
16. 此段台词的意思是：那很好呀，说真话，两位好上尉，如果你们不嫌弃的话，只要有机会，我就来奉陪。那是一定的，没错儿。
17. 此段台词的意思是：天哪，我的双眼还没闭上以前，我还要好好地干一番，要么就是为国家尽忠，战死沙场！大丈夫应视死如归，我就该这样做，总而言之，我就是这么一句话。我的妈，我倒是很想听听你们俩的谈话呢。
18. **Blackheath:** 黑荒原，在伦敦东南部。
19. **the General of our gracious Empress:** 伊丽莎白女王的宠臣埃塞克斯伯爵。
20. **Gallia:** 高卢（西欧古国）。

四、拓展思考

1. Please summarize the main features of the four officers in the selected part. How do you comment on the characterization of the Irish office MacMorris?
2. What do you think of the factual error of conquering Ireland by Earl of Essex in Act V?

3. Please get some background knowledge on the relationship between England and Ireland. Then how does Shakespeare see Ireland according to the selected acts?

五、延展阅读

对大多数读者来说，《罗密欧与朱丽叶》或者《威尼斯商人》是莎士比亚戏剧选读的不二选择。这两部剧本也集中代表和反映了莎士比亚戏剧（喜剧）中的人文主义思想——对传统旧势力的抗争、青年一代对自由和爱情的追求和执着、女性的智慧与热情。当然在主流之外，《威尼斯商人》中的夏洛克形象地塑造了潜藏于那个时代并根植在英格兰作家头脑中的排犹主义。

16世纪90年代是莎士比亚创作历史剧的时代。本篇节选的《亨利五世》最吸引之处在于它描述和呈现了一个英武、足智多谋的英国君王形象。英国对女王的继承人选和对一位圣明君主的呼唤和渴求是强烈的。然而，在主流情节框架下，细心的读者可以看到很多深藏隐约的历史细节：剧中四个军官分别来自英格兰、苏格兰、威尔士、爱尔兰，分别暗示了英国的四个民族。那么，这些虚构的戏剧人物隐含着怎样复杂而敏感的国族关系呢？事实上，从莎翁的历史剧系列中我们可以剥离附着在戏剧文本外面的虚构外壳，搜寻到历史的种种真实。

《亨利五世》向我们展现了英国伊丽莎白时期英格兰纷繁复杂的社会历史、民族关系（尤其是英格兰—苏格兰、英格兰—爱尔兰）和文化心态。对此段历史有兴趣的读者可以系统地阅读莎士比亚的历史剧，看看莎翁的历史剧是如何描述爱尔兰人和爱尔兰民族形象的，并可以将莎翁历史剧中的爱尔兰形象置于16世纪英格兰—爱尔兰民族关系的历史情境下考察，透过文学现象考察现象产生的深层文化动因，从另一个侧面领会莎士比亚戏剧深厚的文化内涵，进一步体会“说不尽的莎士比亚”的意义。

CHAPTER 2

奥斯卡·王尔德

Oscar Wilde

《认真的重要性》

The Importance of Being Earnest

一、剧作家简介

奥斯卡·王尔德（Oscar Wild）1854年生于爱尔兰都柏林的一个家世卓越的家庭。他的父亲是一名外科医生，母亲是一位诗人与作家。1874年，王尔德进入牛津大学学习。在牛津，王尔德受到了沃尔特·佩特（Walter Pater，1839—1894）及约翰·拉斯金（John Ruskin，1819—1900）的审美观念影响，并接触了新黑格尔派哲学、达尔文进化论和拉斐尔前派的作品，这为他之后成为唯美主义先锋作家确立了方向。

王尔德早期作品中的两本童话集：《快乐王子故事集》（*The Happy Prince and Other Tales*，1888）和《石榴之家》（*A House of Pomegranates*，1891），已载入英国儿童文学史册。他在《道林·格雷的画像》（*The Picture of Dorian Gray*，1891）中的序言和论文集《意图》（*Intentions*，1891）中系统地阐述了“为艺术而艺术”的美学观点。他的《温德米尔夫人的扇子》（*Lady Windermere's Fan*，1892）、《莎乐美》（*Salomé*，1893）等戏剧作品堪称一时之绝唱。随后，王尔德接连发表了风俗喜剧《理想的丈夫》（*An Ideal Husband*，1898）等，这些喜剧在演出后颇受欢迎。他于1895年创作的《认真的重要性》（*The Importance of Being Earnest*）被认为是他的代表剧作。他在戏剧中取得的伟大成就在于利用戏剧对话诙谐的语言揭示上层社会的腐朽与混乱。戏剧中很多名言警句甚至来自于一些负面角色，这使对话显得更加有趣，也使人物塑造更加丰满而真实。

王尔德被誉为“才子和戏剧家”，富有过人的自信和天赋。虽然他的晚年极为潦倒，但他的艺术成就仍然使他成为世界经典艺术家，是19世纪与萧伯纳（George Bernard Shaw，1856—1950）齐名的“英国”才子。

1900年，王尔德因脑膜炎于巴黎的一家旅馆去世，终年46岁。

二、剧情简介

《认真的重要性》讲述的是青年绅士约翰和受他监护的未成年女子塞西莉及其家庭女

教师一同住乡下的家中，约翰爱上了伦敦的朋友阿尔杰农的表妹格温多林，因此时常要到伦敦去。为了掩饰自己的行为，他给自己虚构出一个名叫“埃那斯特”的兄弟，以此作为搪塞塞西莉的借口。然而，阿尔杰农也冒充那位并不存在的“埃那斯特”，自称是约翰的兄弟，并且爱上了塞西莉，结果发现塞西莉的女教师就是28年前把布雷克奈尔夫人姐姐的孩子错放在手提箱里的那位粗心的保姆。约翰的真名就叫“埃那斯特”，是阿尔杰农的亲哥哥。最后这两对有情人终成眷属。本选篇节选自该剧第一幕，通过杰克和阿尔杰农两位花花公子诙谐幽默的对话，展现出他们各自的性格。

这是一出聚焦英国上层社会生活的喜剧。其成功之处在于剧作家王尔德在继承社会风尚喜剧传统的基础上，充分发挥运用了机智、诙谐、生动的戏剧语言，展现英国上流社会纵享轻狂的奢靡生活。该戏剧的目的并不在于对19世纪英国维多利亚时代上流社会物质主义享乐展开批判或鞭挞，而主要是通过出其不意的情节布局和机敏中带着的犀利的语言风格营造艺术形式之美。戏剧的关键词Earnest（埃那斯特）既是人名，又双关意指认真，巧妙的转换隐喻了以约翰和阿尔杰农为代表的上流社会青年的双面生活。戏剧的喜剧结局给予了剧中人物命运皆大欢喜式的俗世安排，典型地反映出剧作家不倾现实主义，而慕唯美主义的美学理念——为艺术而艺术。

三、名篇选读

The Importance of Being Earnest

ACT I

SCENE: Morning-room in Algernon's flat in Half-Moon Street. The room is luxuriously and artistically furnished. The sound of a piano is heard in the adjoining room.

(*LANE is arranging afternoon tea on the table, and after the music has ceased, ALGERNON enters.*)

ALGERNON: Did you hear what I was playing, Lane?

LANE: I didn't think it polite to listen, sir.

ALGERNON: I'm sorry for that, for your sake. I don't play accurately—any one can play accurately—but I play with wonderful expression.

As far as the piano is concerned, sentiment is my forte. I keep science for Life.[1]

LANE: Yes, sir.

ALGERNON: And, speaking of the science of Life, have you got the cucumber sandwiches cut for Lady Bracknell?

LANE: Yes, sir. (*hands them on a salver.*)

ALGERNON: (*inspects them, takes two, and sits down on the sofa*) Oh!... By the way, Lane, I see from your book that on Thursday night, when Lord Shoreman and Mr. Worthing were dining with me, eight bottles of champagne are entered as having been consumed.

LANE: Yes, sir; eight bottles and a pint.

ALGERNON: Why is it that at a bachelor's establishment the servants invariably drink the champagne? I ask merely for information.

LANE: I attribute it to the superior quality of the wine, sir. I have often observed that in married households the champagne is rarely of a first-rate brand.

ALGERNON: Good heavens! Is marriage so demoralizing as that?

LANE: I believe it is a very pleasant state, sir. I have had very little experience of it myself up to the present. I have only been married once. That was in consequence of a misunderstanding between myself and a young person.

ALGERNON: (*languidly*) I don't know that I am much interested in your family life, Lane.

LANE: No, sir; it is not a very interesting subject. I never think of it myself.

ALGERNON: Very natural, I am sure. That will do, Lane, thank you.

LANE: Thank you, sir.

(*LANE goes out.*)

ALGERNON: Lane's views on marriage seem somewhat lax. Really, if the lower orders[2] don't set us a good example, what on earth is the use of them? They seem, as a class, to have absolutely no sense of moral responsibility.

(*enter LANE*)

LANE: Mr. Ernest Worthing.

(*enter JACK*)

(*lANE goes out.*)

ALGERNON: How are you, my dear Ernest? What brings you up to town?

JACK: Oh, pleasure, pleasure! What else should bring one anywhere?[3] Eating as usual, I see, Algy!

ALGERNON: (*stiffly*) I believe it is customary in good society to take some slight refreshment at five o'clock. Where have you been since last Thursday?

JACK: (*sitting down on the sofa*) In the country.

ALGERNON: What on earth do you do there?

JACK: (*pulling off his gloves*) When one is in town one amuses oneself. When one is in the country one amuses other people.[4] It is excessively boring.

ALGERNON: And who are the people you amuse?

JACK: (*airily*) Oh, neighbours, neighbours.

ALGERNON: Got nice neighbours in your part of Shropshire?

JACK: Perfectly horrid! Never speak to one of them.

ALGERNON: How immensely you must amuse them! (*goes over and takes sandwich*) By the way, Shropshire is your county, is it not?

JACK: Eh? Shropshire? Yes, of course. Hallo! Why all these cups? Why cucumber sandwiches? Why such reckless extravagance in one so young? Who is coming to tea? [5]

ALGERNON: Oh! Merely Aunt Augusta and Gwendolen.

JACK: How perfectly delightful!

ALGERNON: Yes, that is all very well; but I am afraid Aunt Augusta won't quite approve of your being here.

JACK: May I ask why?

ALGERNON: My dear fellow, the way you flirt with Gwendolen is perfectly disgraceful. It is almost as bad as the way Gwendolen flirts with you.

JACK: I am in love with Gwendolen. I have come up to town expressly to propose to her.

ALGERNON: I thought you had come up for pleasure?... I call that business.

JACK: How utterly unromantic you are!

ALGERNON: I really don't see anything romantic in proposing. It is very romantic to be in love. But there is nothing romantic about a definite proposal. Why, one may be accepted. One usually is, I believe. Then the excitement is all over. The very essence of romance is uncertainty. If ever I get married, I'll certainly try to forget the fact.

JACK: I have no doubt about that, dear Algy. The Divorce Court was specially invented for people whose memories are so curiously constituted.[6]

ALGERNON: Oh! There is no use speculating on that subject. Divorces are made in Heaven—(*JACK puts out his hand to take a sandwich. ALGERNON at once interferes.*) Please don't touch the cucumber sandwiches. They are ordered specially for Aunt Augusta. (*takes one and eats it*)

JACK: Well, you have been eating them all the time.

ALGERNON: That is quite a different matter. She is my aunt. (*takes plate from below*) Have some bread and butter. The bread and butter is for Gwendolen. Gwendolen is devoted to bread and butter.

JACK: (*advancing to table and helping himself*) And very good bread and butter it is too.

ALGERNON: Well, my dear fellow, you need not eat as if you were going to eat it all. You behave as if you were married to her already. You are not married to her already, and I don't think you ever will be.

JACK: Why on earth do you say that?

ALGERNON: Well, in the first place girls never marry the men they flirt with. Girls don't think it right.[7]

JACK: Oh, that is nonsense!

ALGERNON: It isn't. It is a great truth. It accounts for the extraordinary number of bachelors that one sees all over the place. In the second place, I don't give my consent.

JACK: Your consent!

ALGERNON: My dear fellow, Gwendolen is my first cousin. And before I allow you to marry her, you will have to clear up the whole question of Cecily.

(*rings bell*)

JACK: Cecily! What on earth do you mean? What do you mean, Algy, by Cecily! I don't know any one of the name of Cecily.

(*enter LANE*)

ALGERNON: Bring me that cigarette case Mr. Worthing left in the smoking-room the last time he dined here.

LANE: Yes, sir.

(*LANE goes out.*)

JACK: Do you mean to say you have had my cigarette case all this time? I wish to goodness you had let me know. I have been writing frantic letters to Scotland Yard [8]about it. I was very nearly offering a large reward.

ALGERNON: Well, I wish you would offer one. I happen to be more than usually hard up.

JACK: There is no good offering a large reward now that the thing is found.

(*enter LANE with the cigarette case on a salver; ALGERNON takes it at once. LANE goes out.*)

ALGERNON: I think that is rather mean of you, Ernest, I must say. (*opens case and examines it*) However, it makes no matter, for, now that I look at the inscription inside, I find that the thing isn't yours after all.

JACK: Of course it's mine. (*moving to him*) You have seen me with it a hundred times, and you have no right whatsoever to read what is written inside. It is a very ungentlemanly thing to read a private cigarette case.

ALGERNON: Oh! It is absurd to have a hard and fast rule about what one should read and what one shouldn't. More than half of modern culture depends on what one shouldn't read.

JACK: I am quite aware of the fact, and I don't propose to discuss modern culture. It isn't the sort of thing one should talk of in private. I simply want my cigarette case back.

ALGERNON: Yes, but this isn't your cigarette case. This cigarette case is a present from some one of the name of Cecily, and you said you didn't know any one of that name.

JACK: Well, if you want to know, Cecily happens to be my aunt.

ALGERNON: Your aunt!

JACK: Yes. Charming old lady she is, too. Lives at Tunbridge Wells. Just give it back to me, Algy.

ALGERNON: (*retreating to back of sofa*) But why does she call herself little Cecily if she is your aunt and lives at Tunbridge Wells? (*reading*) "From little Cecily with her fondest love."

JACK: (*moving to sofa and kneeling upon it*) My dear fellow, what on earth is there in that? Some aunts are tall, and some aunts are not tall. That is a matter that surely an aunt may be allowed to decide for herself. You seem to think that every aunt should be exactly like your aunt! That is absurd! For Heaven's sake give me back my cigarette case.

(*follows ALGERNON round the room*)

ALGERNON: Yes. But why does your aunt call you her uncle? 'From little Cecily, with her fondest love to her dear Uncle Jack.' There is no objection, I admit, to an aunt being a small aunt, but why an aunt, no matter what her size may be, should call her own nephew her uncle; I can't quite make out. Besides, your name isn't Jack at all; it is Ernest.

JACK: It isn't Ernest; it's Jack.

ALGERNON: You have always told me it was Ernest. I have introduced you to every one as Ernest. You answer to the name of Ernest. You look as if your name was Ernest. You are the most earnest-looking person I ever saw in my life. It is perfectly absurd your saying that your name isn't Ernest. It's on your cards. Here is one of them. (*taking it from case*) 'Mr. Ernest Worthing, B. 4, The Albany.' I'll keep this as a proof that your name is Ernest if ever you attempt to deny it to me, or to Gwendolen, or to any one else. (*puts the card in his pocket*)

JACK: Well, my name is Ernest in town and Jack in the country, and the cigarette case was given to me in the country.

ALGERNON: Yes, but that does not account for the fact that your small Aunt Cecily, who lives at Tunbridge Wells, calls you her dear uncle. Come, old boy, you had much better have the thing out at once.

JACK: My dear Algy, you talk exactly as if you were a dentist. It is very vulgar to talk like a dentist when one isn't a dentist. It produces a false impression.

ALGERNON: Well, that is exactly what dentists always do. Now, go on! Tell me the whole thing. I may mention that I have always suspected you of being a confirmed and secret Bunburyist; and I am quite sure of it now.

JACK: Bunburyist? What on earth do you mean by a Bunburyist?

ALGERNON: I'll reveal to you the meaning of that incomparable expression as soon as you are kind enough to inform me why you are Ernest in town and Jack in the country.

JACK: Well, produce my cigarette case first.

ALGERNON: Here it is. (*hands cigarette case*) Now produce your explanation, and pray make it improbable. (*sits on sofa*)

JACK: My dear fellow, there is nothing improbable about my explanation at all. In fact it's perfectly ordinary. Old Mr. Thomas

Cardew, who adopted me when I was a little boy, made me in his will guardian to his grand-daughter, Miss Cecily Cardew. Cecily, who addresses me as her uncle from motives of respect that you could not possibly appreciate, lives at my place in the country under the charge of her admirable governess, Miss Prism.

ALGERNON: Where in that place in the country, by the way?

JACK: That is nothing to you, dear boy. You are not going to be invited... I may tell you candidly that the place is not in Shropshire[9].

ALGERNON: I suspected that, my dear fellow! I have Bunburyed all over Shropshire on two separate occasions. Now, go on. Why are you Ernest in town and Jack in the country?

JACK: My dear Algy, I don't know whether you will be able to understand my real motives. You are hardly serious enough. When one is placed in the position of guardian, one has to adopt a very high moral tone on all subjects. It's one's duty to do so. And as a high moral tone can hardly be said to conduce very much to either one's health or one's happiness, in order to get up to town I have always pretended to have a younger brother of the name of Ernest, who lives in the Albany, and gets into the most dreadful scrapes. That, my dear Algy, is the whole truth pure and simple.

ALGERNON: The truth is rarely pure and never simple. Modern life would be very tedious if it were either, and modern literature a complete impossibility!

JACK: That wouldn't be at all a bad thing.

ALGERNON: Literary criticism is not your forte, my dear fellow. Don't try it. You should leave that to people who haven't been at a University. They do it so well in the daily papers. What you really are is a Bunburyist. I was quite right in saying you were a Bunburyist. You are one of the most advanced Bunburyists I know.

JACK: What on earth do you mean?

ALGERNON: You have invented a very useful younger brother called Ernest, in order that you may be able to come up to town as often as you like. I have invented an invaluable permanent invalid called Bunbury, in order that I may be able to go down into the country whenever I choose. Bunbury is perfectly invaluable. If it wasn't for Bunbury's extraordinary bad health, for instance, I wouldn't be able to dine with you at Willis's to-night, for I have been really engaged to Aunt Augusta for more than a week.

JACK: I haven't asked you to dine with me anywhere to-night.

ALGERNON: I know. You are absurdly careless about sending out invitations. It is very foolish of you. Nothing annoys people so much as not receiving invitations.

JACK: You had much better dine with your Aunt Augusta.

ALGERNON: I haven't the smallest intention of doing anything of the kind. To begin with, I dined there on Monday, and once a week is quite enough to dine with one's own relations. In the second place, whenever I do dine there I am always treated as a member of the family, and sent down with either no woman at all, or two. In the third place, I know perfectly well whom she will place me next to, to-night. She will place me next Mary Farquhar, who always flirts with her own husband across the dinner-table. That is not very pleasant. Indeed, it is not even decent... and that sort of thing is enormously on the increase. The amount of women in London who flirt with their own husbands is perfectly scandalous. It looks so bad. It is simply washing one's clean linen in public[10]. Besides, now that I know you to be a confirmed Bunburyist I naturally want to talk to you about Bunburying. I want to tell you the rules.

JACK: I'm not a Bunburyist at all. If Gwendolen accepts me, I am going to kill my brother, indeed I think I'll kill him in any case. Cecily is a little too much interested in him. It is rather a bore. So I am going to get rid of Ernest. And I strongly advise you to do the same with Mr.... with your invalid friend who has the absurd name.

ALGERNON: Nothing will induce me to part with Bunbury, and if you ever get married, which seems to me extremely problematic, you will be very glad to know Bunbury. A man who marries without knowing Bunbury has a very tedious time of it.

JACK: That is nonsense. If I marry a charming girl like Gwendolen, and she is the only girl I ever saw in my life that I would marry, I certainly won't want to know Bunbury.

ALGERNON: Then your wife will. You don't seem to realise, that in married life three is company and two is none[11].

JACK: (*sententiously*) That, my dear young friend, is the theory that the corrupt French Drama has been propounding for the last fifty years.

ALGERNON: Yes, and that the happy English home has proved in half the time.

JACK: For heaven's sake, don't try to be cynical. It's perfectly easy to be cynical.

ALGERNON: My dear fellow, it isn't easy to be anything nowadays. There's such a lot of beastly competition about. (*The sound of an electric bell is heard.*) Ah! that must be Aunt Augusta. Only relatives, or creditors, ever ring in that Wagnerian[12] manner. Now, if I get her out of the way for ten minutes, so that you can have an opportunity for proposing to Gwendolen, may I dine with you to-night at Willis's?

JACK: I suppose so, if you want to.

ALGERNON: Yes, but you must be serious about it. I hate people who are not serious about meals. It is so shallow of them.

(*enter LANE*)

LANE: Lady Bracknell and Miss Fairfax.

(*ALGERNON goes forward to meet them. Enter LADY BRACKNELL and GWENDOLEN.*)

LADY BRACKNELL: Good afternoon, dear Algernon, I hope you are behaving very well.

ALGERNON: I'm feeling very well, Aunt Augusta.

LADY BRACKNELL: That's not quite the same thing. In fact the two things rarely go together. (*sees JACK and bows to him with icy coldness*)

ALGERNON: (*to GWENDOLEN*) Dear me, you are smart!

GWENDOLEN: I am always smart! Am I not, Mr. Worthing?

JACK: You're quite perfect, Miss Fairfax.

GWENDOLEN: Oh! I hope I am not that. It would leave no room for developments, and I intend to develop in many directions. (*GWENDOLEN and JACK sit down together in the corner.*)

LADY BRACKNELL: I'm sorry if we are a little late, Algernon, but I was obliged to call on dear Lady Harbury. I hadn't been there since her poor husband's death. I never saw a woman so altered; she looks quite twenty years younger. And now I'll have a cup of tea, and one of those nice cucumber sandwiches you promised me.

ALGERNON: Certainly, Aunt Augusta. (*goes over to tea-table*)

LADY BRACKNELL: Won't you come and sit here, Gwendolen?

GWENDOLEN: Thanks, mamma, I'm quite comfortable where I am.

ALGERNON: (*picking up empty plate in horror*) Good heavens! Lane! Why are there no cucumber sandwiches? I ordered them specially.

LANE: (*gravely*) There were no cucumbers in the market this morning, sir. I went down twice.

ALGERNON: No cucumbers!

LANE: No, sir. Not even for ready money.

ALGERNON: That will do, Lane, thank you.

LANE: Thank you, sir. (*goes out*)

ALGERNON: I am greatly distressed, Aunt Augusta, about there being no cucumbers, not even for ready money.

LADY BRACKNELL: It really makes no matter, Algernon. I had some crumpets with Lady Harbury, who seems to me to be living entirely for pleasure now.

ALGERNON: I hear her hair has turned quite gold from grief.

LADY BRACKNELL: It certainly has changed its colour. From what cause I, of course, cannot say. (*ALGERNON crosses and hands tea.*) Thank you. I've quite a treat for you to-night, Algernon. I am going to send you down with Mary Farquhar. She is such a nice woman, and so attentive to her husband. It's delightful to watch them.

ALGERNON: I am afraid, Aunt Augusta. I shall have to give up the pleasure of dining with you to-night after all.

LADY BRACKNELL: (*frowning*) I hope not, Algernon. It would put my table completely out. Your uncle would have to dine upstairs. Fortunately he is accustomed to that.

ALGERNON: It is a great bore, and I need hardly say, a terrible disappointment to me, but the fact is I have just had a telegram to say that my poor friend Bunbury is very ill again. (*exchanges glances with JACK*) They seem to think I should be with him.

LADY BRACKNELL: It is very strange. This Mr. Bunbury seems to suffer from curiously bad health.

ALGERNON: Yes; poor Bunbury is a dreadful invalid.

LADY BRACKNELL: Well, I must say, Algernon, that I think it is high time that Mr. Bunbury made up his mind whether he was going to live or to die. This shilly-shallying with the question is absurd. Nor do I in any way approve of the modern sympathy with invalids. I consider it morbid. Illness of any kind is hardly a thing to be encouraged in others. Health is the primary duty of life. I am always telling that to your poor uncle, but he never seems to take much notice... as far as any improvement in his ailment goes. I should be much obliged if you would ask Mr. Bunbury, from me, to be kind enough not to have a relapse on Saturday, for I rely on you to arrange my music for me. It is my last reception, and one wants something that will encourage conversation, particularly at the end of the season when every one has practically said whatever they had to say, which, in most cases, was probably not much.

ALGERNON: I'll speak to Bunbury, Aunt Augusta, if he is still conscious, and I think I can promise you he'll be all right by Saturday. Of course the music is a great difficulty. You see, if one plays good music, people don't listen, and if one plays bad music people don't talk. But I'll run over the programme I've drawn out, if you will kindly come into the next room for a moment.

LADY BRACKNELL: Thank you, Algernon. It is very thoughtful of you. (*rising, and following ALGERNON*) I'm sure the programme will be delightful, after a few expurgations. French songs I cannot possibly allow. People always seem to think that they are improper, and either look shocked, which is vulgar, or laugh, which is worse. But German sounds a thoroughly respectable language, and indeed, I believe is so. Gwendolen, you will accompany me.

GWENDOLEN: Certainly, mamma.

(*LADY BRACKNELL and ALGERNON go into the music-room, GWENDOLEN remains behind.*)

JACK: Charming day it has been, Miss Fairfax.

GWENDOLEN: Pray don't talk to me about the weather, Mr. Worthing. Whenever people talk to me about the weather, I always feel quite certain that they mean something else. And that makes me so nervous.

JACK: I do mean something else.

GWENDOLEN: I thought so. In fact, I am never wrong.

JACK: And I would like to be allowed to take advantage of Lady Bracknell's temporary absence...

GWENDOLEN: I would certainly advise you to do so. Mamma has a way of coming back suddenly into a room that I have often had to speak to her about.

JACK: (*nervously*) Miss Fairfax, ever since I met you I have admired you more than any girl... I have ever met since... I met you.

GWENDOLEN: Yes, I am quite well aware of the fact. And I often wish that in public, at any rate, you had been more demonstrative. For me you have always had an irresistible fascination. Even before I met you I was far from indifferent to you. (*JACK looks at her in amazement.*) We live, as I hope you know, Mr. Worthing, in an age of ideals. The fact is constantly mentioned in the more expensive monthly magazines, and has reached the provincial pulpits, I am told; and my ideal has always been to love some one of the name of Ernest. There is something in that name that inspires absolute confidence. The moment Algernon first mentioned to me that he had a friend called Ernest, I knew I was destined to love you.

JACK: You really love me, Gwendolen?

GWENDOLEN: Passionately!

JACK: Darling! You don't know how happy you've made me.

GWENDOLEN: My own Ernest!

JACK: But you don't really mean to say that you couldn't love me if my name wasn't Ernest?

GWENDOLEN: But your name is Ernest.

JACK: Yes, I know it is. But supposing it was something else? Do you mean to say you couldn't love me then?

GWENDOLEN: (*glibly*) Ah! that is clearly a metaphysical speculation, and like most metaphysical speculations has very little reference at all to the actual facts of real life, as we know them.

JACK: Personally, darling, to speak quite candidly, I don't much care about the name of Ernest... I don't think the name suits me at all.

GWENDOLEN: It suits you perfectly. It is a divine name. It has a music of its own. It produces vibrations.

JACK: Well, really, Gwendolen, I must say that I think there are lots of other much nicer names. I think Jack, for instance, a charming name.

GWENDOLEN: Jack?... No, there is very little music in the name Jack, if any at all, indeed. It does not thrill. It produces absolutely no vibrations... I have known several Jacks, and they all, without exception, were more than usually plain. Besides, Jack is a notorious domesticity for John! And I pity any woman who is married to a man called John. She would probably never be allowed to know the entrancing pleasure of a single moment's solitude. The only really safe name is Ernest.

JACK: Gwendolen, I must get christened at once—I mean we must get married at once. There is no time to be lost.

GWENDOLEN: Married, Mr. Worthing?

JACK: (*astounded*) Well... surely. You know that I love you, and you led me to believe, Miss Fairfax, that you were not absolutely indifferent to me.

GWENDOLEN: I adore you. But you haven't proposed to me yet. Nothing has been said at all about marriage. The subject has not even been touched on.

JACK: Well... may I propose to you now?

GWENDOLEN: I think it would be an admirable opportunity. And to spare you any possible disappointment, Mr. Worthing, I think it only fair to tell you quite frankly before-hand that I am fully determined to accept you.

JACK: Gwendolen!

GWENDOLEN: Yes, Mr. Worthing, what have you got to say to me?

JACK: You know what I have got to say to you.

GWENDOLEN: Yes, but you don't say it.

JACK: Gwendolen, will you marry me? (*goes on his knees*)

GWENDOLEN: Of course I will, darling. How long you have been about it! I am afraid you have had very little experience in how to propose.

JACK: My own one, I have never loved any one in the world but you.

GWENDOLEN: Yes, but men often propose for practice. I know my brother

Gerald does. All my girl-friends tell me so. What wonderfully blue eyes you have, Ernest! They are quite, quite, blue. I hope you will always look at me just like that, especially when there are other people present.

(*enter LADY BRACKNELL*)

LADY BRACKNELL: Mr. Worthing! Rise, sir, from this semi-recumbent posture. It is most indecorous.

GWENDOLEN: Mamma! (*He tries to rise; she restrains him.*) I must beg you to retire. This is no place for you. Besides, Mr. Worthing has not quite finished yet.

LADY BRACKNELL: Finished what, may I ask?

GWENDOLEN: I am engaged to Mr. Worthing, mamma. (*They rise together.*)

LADY BRACKNELL: Pardon me, you are not engaged to any one. When you do become engaged to some one, I, or your father, should his health permit him, will inform you of the fact. An engagement should come on a young girl as a surprise, pleasant or unpleasant, as the case may be. It is hardly a matter that she could be allowed to arrange for herself... And now I have a few questions to put to you, Mr. Worthing. While I am making these inquiries, you, Gwendolen, will wait for me below in the carriage.

GWENDOLEN: (*reproachfully*) Mamma!

LADY BRACKNELL: In the carriage, Gwendolen! (*GWENDOLEN goes to the door. She and JACK blow kisses to each other behind LADY BRACKNELL'S back. LADY BRACKNELL looks vaguely about as if she could not understand what the noise was. Finally turns round*) Gwendolen, the carriage!

GWENDOLEN: Yes, mamma. (*goes out, looking back at JACK*)

LADY BRACKNELL: (*sitting down*) You can take a seat, Mr. Worthing. (*Looks in her pocket for note-book and pencil*)

JACK: Thank you, Lady Bracknell, I prefer standing.

LADY BRACKNELL: (*pencil and note-book in hand*) I feel bound to tell you that you are not down on my list of eligible young men, although I have the same list as the dear Duchess of Bolton has. We work together, in fact. However, I am quite ready to enter your name, should your answers be what a really affectionate mother requires. Do you smoke?

JACK: Well, yes, I must admit I smoke.

LADY BRACKNELL: I am glad to hear it. A man should always have an occupation of some kind. There are far too many idle men in London as it is. How old are you?

JACK: Twenty-nine.

LADY BRACKNELL: A very good age to be married at. I have always been of opinion that a man who desires to get married should know either everything or nothing. Which do you know?

JACK: (*after some hesitation*) I know nothing, Lady Bracknell.

LADY BRACKNELL: I am pleased to hear it. I do not approve of anything that tampers with natural ignorance. Ignorance is like a delicate exotic fruit; touch it and the bloom is gone. The whole theory of modern education is radically unsound. Fortunately in England, at any rate, education produces no effect whatsoever. If it did, it would prove a serious danger to the upper classes, and probably lead to acts of violence in Grosvenor Square. What is your income?

JACK: Between seven and eight thousand a year.

LADY BRACKNELL: (*makes a note in her book*) In land, or in investments?

JACK: In investments, chiefly.

LADY BRACKNELL: That is satisfactory. What between the duties expected of one during one's lifetime, and the duties exacted from one after one's death, land has ceased to be either a profit or a pleasure. It gives one position, and prevents one from keeping it up. That's all that can be said about land.

JACK: I have a country house with some land, of course, attached to it, about fifteen hundred acres, I believe; but I don't depend on that for my real income. In fact, as far as I can make out, the poachers are the only people who make anything out of it.

LADY BRACKNELL: A country house! How many bedrooms? Well, that point can be cleared up afterwards. You have a town house, I hope? A girl with a simple, unspoiled nature, like Gwendolen, could hardly be expected to reside in the country.

JACK: Well, I own a house in Belgrave Square[13], but it is let by the year to Lady Bloxham. Of course, I can get it back whenever I like, at six months' notice.

LADY BRACKNELL: Lady Bloxham? I don't know her.

JACK: Oh, she goes about very little. She is a lady considerably advanced in years.

LADY BRACKNELL: Ah, nowadays that is no guarantee of respectability of character. What number in Belgrave Square?

JACK: 149.

LADY BRACKNELL: (*shaking her head*) The unfashionable side. I thought there was something.

However, that could easily be altered.

JACK: Do you mean the fashion, or the side?

LADY BRACKNELL: (*sternly*) Both, if necessary, I presume. What are your polities?

JACK: Well, I am afraid I really have none. I am a Liberal Unionist.

LADY BRACKNELL: Oh, they count as Tories. They dine with us. Or come in the evening, at any rate. Now to minor matters. Are your parents living?

JACK: I have lost both my parents.

LADY BRACKNELL: To lose one parent, Mr. Worthing, may be regarded as a misfortune; to lose both looks like carelessness. Who was your father? He was evidently a man of some wealth. Was he born in what the Radical papers call the purple of commerce, or did he rise from the ranks of the aristocracy?

JACK: I am afraid I really don't know. The fact is, Lady Bracknell, I said I had lost my parents. It would be nearer the truth to say that my parents seem to have lost me... I don't actually know

	who I am by birth. I was... well, I was found.
LADY BRACKNELL:	Found!
JACK:	The late Mr. Thomas Cardew, an old gentleman of a very charitable and kindly disposition, found me, and gave me the name of Worthing, because he happened to have a first-class ticket for Worthing in his pocket at the time. Worthing is a place in Sussex. It is a seaside resort.
LADY BRACKNELL:	Where did the charitable gentleman who had a first-class ticket for this seaside resort find you?
JACK:	(*gravely*) In a hand-bag.
LADY BRACKNELL:	A hand-bag?
JACK:	(*very seriously*) Yes, Lady Bracknell. I was in a hand-bag—a somewhat large, black leather hand-bag, with handles to it—an ordinary hand-bag in fact.
LADY BRACKNELL:	In what locality did this Mr. James, or Thomas Cardew come across this ordinary hand-bag?
JACK:	In the cloak-room at Victoria Station. It was given to him in mistake for his own.
LADY BRACKNELL:	The cloak-room at Victoria Station?
JACK:	Yes. The Brighton line.
LADY BRACKNELL:	The line is immaterial. Mr. Worthing, I confess I feel somewhat bewildered by what you have just told me. To be born, or at any rate bred, in a hand-bag, whether it had handles or not, seems to me to display a contempt for the ordinary decencies of family life that reminds one of the worst excesses of the French Revolution. And I presume you know what that unfortunate movement led to? As for the particular locality in which the hand-bag was found, a cloak-room at a railway station might serve to conceal a social indiscretion—has probably, indeed, been used for that purpose before now—but it could hardly be regarded as an assured basis for a recognised position in good society.

JACK: May I ask you then what you would advise me to do? I need hardly say I would do anything in the world to ensure Gwendolen's happiness.

LADY BRACKNELL: I would strongly advise you, Mr. Worthing, to try and acquire some relations as soon as possible, and to make a definite effort to produce at any rate one parent, of either sex, before the season is quite over.

JACK: Well, I don't see how I could possibly manage to do that. I can produce the hand-bag at any moment. It is in my dressing-room at home. I really think that should satisfy you, Lady Bracknell.

LADY BRACKNELL: Me, sir! What has it to do with me? You can hardly imagine that I and Lord Bracknell would dream of allowing our only daughter—a girl brought up with the utmost care—to marry into a cloak-room, and form an alliance with a parcel? Good morning, Mr. Worthing!

(*LADY BRACKNELL sweeps out in majestic indignation.*)

JACK: Good morning! (*ALGERNON, from the other room, strikes up the Wedding March. JACK looks perfectly furious, and goes to the door.*) For goodness' sake don't play that ghastly tune, Algy. How idiotic you are! (*The music stops and ALGERNON enters cheerily.*)

ALGERNON: Didn't it go off all right, old boy? You don't mean to say Gwendolen refused you? I know it is a way she has. She is always refusing people. I think it is most ill-natured of her.

JACK: Oh, Gwendolen is as right as a trivet[14]. As far as she is concerned, we are engaged. Her mother is perfectly unbearable. Never met such a Gorgon[15]... I don't really know what a Gorgon is like, but I am quite sure that Lady Bracknell is one. In any case, she is a monster, without being a myth, which is rather unfair... I beg your pardon, Algy. I suppose I shouldn't talk about your own aunt in that way before you.

ALGERNON: My dear boy, I love hearing my relations abused. It is the only thing that makes me put up with them at all. Relations are simply a tedious pack of people, who haven't got the remotest knowledge of how to live, nor the smallest instinct about when to die.

JACK: Oh, that is nonsense!

ALGERNON: It isn't!

JACK: Well, I won't argue about the matter. You always want to argue about things.

ALGERNON: That is exactly what things were originally made for.

JACK: Upon my word, if I thought that, I'd shoot myself... (a pause) You don't think there is any chance of Gwendolen becoming like her mother in about a hundred and fifty years, do you, Algy?

ALGERNON: All women become like their mothers. That is their tragedy. No man does. That's his.

JACK: Is that clever?

ALGERNON: It is perfectly phrased, and quite as true as any observation in civilised life should be.

JACK: I am sick to death of cleverness. Everybody is clever nowadays. You can't go anywhere without meeting clever people. The thing has become an absolute public nuisance. I wish to goodness we had a few fools left.

ALGERNON: We have.

JACK: I should extremely like to meet them. What do they talk about?

ALGERNON: The fools? Oh! About the clever people, of course.

JACK: What fools!

ALGERNON: By the way, did you tell Gwendolen the truth about your being Ernest in town, and Jack in the country?

JACK: (*in a very patronising manner*) My dear fellow, the truth isn't quite the sort of thing one tells to a nice, sweet, refined girl. What extraordinary ideas you have about the way to behave to a woman!

ALGERNON: The only way to behave to a woman is to make love to her, if she is pretty, and to some one else, if she is plain.

JACK:	Oh, that is nonsense.
ALGERNON:	What about your brother? What about the profligate Ernest?
JACK:	Oh, before the end of the week I shall have got rid of him. I'll say he died in Paris of apoplexy. Lots of people die of apoplexy, quite suddenly, don't they?
ALGERNON:	Yes, but it's hereditary, my dear fellow. It's a sort of thing that runs in families. You had much better say a severe chill.
JACK:	You are sure a severe chill isn't hereditary, or anything of that kind?
ALGERNON:	Of course it isn't!
JACK:	Very well, then. My poor brother Ernest to carried off suddenly, in Paris, by a severe chill. That gets rid of him.
ALGERNON:	But I thought you said that... Miss Cardew was a little too much interested in your poor brother Ernest? Won't she feel his loss a good deal?
JACK:	Oh, that is all right. Cecily is not a silly romantic girl, I am glad to say. She has got a capital appetite, goes long walks, and pays no attention at all to her lessons.
ALGERNON:	I would rather like to see Cecily.
JACK:	I will take very good care you never do. She is excessively pretty, and she is only just eighteen.
ALGERNON:	Have you told Gwendolen yet that you have an excessively pretty ward who is only just eighteen?
JACK:	Oh! One doesn't blurt these things out to people. Cecily and Gwendolen are perfectly certain to be extremely great friends. I'll bet you anything you like that half an hour after they have met, they will be calling each other sister.
ALGERNON:	Women only do that when they have called each other a lot of other things first. Now, my dear boy, if we want to get a good table at Willis's, we really must go and dress. Do you know it is nearly seven?
JACK:	(*irritably*) Oh! It always is nearly seven.

ALGERNON: Well, I'm hungry.

JACK: I never knew you when you weren't...

ALGERNON: What shall we do after dinner? Go to a theatre?

JACK: Oh no! I loathe listening.

ALGERNON: Well, let us go to the Club?

JACK: Oh, no! I hate talking.

ALGERNON: Well, we might trot round to the Empire at ten?

JACK: Oh, no! I can't bear looking at things. It is so silly.

ALGERNON: Well, what shall we do?

JACK: Nothing!

ALGERNON: It is awfully hard work doing nothing. However, I don't mind hard work where there is no definite object of any kind.

(*enter LANE*)

LANE: Miss Fairfax.

(*enter GWENDOLEN; LANE goes out.*)

ALGERNON: Gwendolen, upon my word!

GWENDOLEN: Algy, kindly turn your back. I have something very particular to say to Mr. Worthing.

ALGERNON: Really, Gwendolen, I don't think I can allow this at all.

GWENDOLEN: Algy, you always adopt a strictly immoral attitude towards life. You are not quite old enough to do that.

(*ALGERNON retires to the fireplace.*)

JACK: My own darling!

GWENDOLEN: Ernest, we may never be married. From the expression on mamma's face I fear we never shall. Few parents nowadays pay any regard to what their children say to them. The old-fashioned respect for the young is fast dying out. Whatever influence I ever had over mamma, I lost at the age of three. But although she may prevent us from becoming man and wife, and I may marry some one else, and marry often, nothing that she can possibly do can alter my eternal devotion to you.

JACK: Dear Gwendolen!

GWENDOLEN: The story of your romantic origin, as related to me by mamma, with unpleasing comments, has naturally stirred the deeper fibres of my nature. Your Christian name has an irresistible fascination. The simplicity of your character makes you exquisitely incomprehensible to me. Your town address at the Albany I have. What is your address in the country?

JACK: The Manor House, Woolton, Hertfordshire.

(*ALGERNON, who has been carefully listening, smiles to himself, and writes the address on his shirt-cuff. Then picks up the Railway Guide.*)

GWENDOLEN: There is a good postal service, I suppose? It may be necessary to do something desperate. That of course will require serious consideration. I will communicate with you daily.

JACK: My own one!

GWENDOLEN: How long do you remain in town?

JACK: Till Monday.

GWENDOLEN: Good! Algy, you may turn round now.

ALGERNON: Thanks, I've turned round already.

GWENDOLEN: You may also ring the bell.

JACK: You will let me see you to your carriage, my own darling?

GWENDOLEN: Certainly.

JACK: (*to LANE, who now enters*) I will see Miss Fairfax out.

LANE: Yes, sir.

(*JACK and GWENDOLEN go off.*)

(*LANE presents several letters on a salver to ALGERNON. It is to be surmised that they are bills, as ALGERNON, after looking at the envelopes, tears them up.*)

ALGERNON: A glass of sherry, Lane.

LANE: Yes, sir.

ALGERNON: To-morrow, Lane, I'm going Bunburying.

LANE:	Yes, sir.
ALGERNON:	I shall probably not be back till Monday. You can put up my dress clothes, my smoking jacket, and all the Bunbury suits...
LANE:	Yes, sir. (*handing sherry*)
ALGERNON:	I hope to-morrow will be a fine day, Lane.
LANE:	It never is, sir.
ALGERNON:	Lane, you're a perfect pessimist.
LANE:	I do my best to give satisfaction, sir.
	(*enter JACK. LANE goes off*)
JACK:	There's a sensible, intellectual girl! The only girl I ever cared for in my life. (*ALGERNON is laughing immoderately.*) What on earth are you so amused at?
ALGERNON:	Oh, I'm a little anxious about poor Bunbury, that in all.
JACK:	If you don't take care, your friend Bunbury will get you into a serious scrape some day.
ALGERNON:	I love scrapes. They are the only things that are never serious.
JACK:	Oh, that's nonsense, Algy. You never talk anything but nonsense.
ALGERNON:	Nobody ever does.
	(*JACK looks indignantly at him, and leaves the room. ALGERNON lights a cigarette, reads his shirt-cuff, and smiles.*)

注释

1. 此处刻画了阿尔杰农试图掩盖他拙劣的弹琴技巧，并揭露了阿尔杰农的虚伪。
2. **the lower orders:** 下层阶级。
3. 这里两个pleasure的反复集中突出了杰克这一花花公子只想着吃喝玩乐的心态，并暗含了一种不以为耻，反以为荣的感觉。
4. 此处台词意思是：在城里时是自己寻开心，在乡下时是让别人寻开心。这个对偶句揭示出杰克游戏人生的态度。
5. 作者在此处使用了省略，一方面，能将生活中的真实情景展现在读者面前；另一方面，这句话是阿尔杰农追问杰克住哪里时说的，将杰克想迅速转换话题时的心虚描绘得淋漓尽致。

6. 这段台词听起来很有道理，但从杰克口中说出，具有很强的讽刺和喜剧效果。

7. 这段台词看似赞扬维多利亚时代的女孩遵守婚姻道德，实则表示她们轻浮、放荡。

8. **Scotland Yard:** 苏格兰场（New Scotland Yard，又称Scotland Yard、The Yard），是英国伦敦警察厅的代称。伦敦警察厅（Metropolitan Police Service，伦敦警方中文官网的名称则为伦敦都市警部）负责包括整个大伦敦地区（伦敦市除外）在内的治安及交通维持。苏格兰场位于伦敦的威斯敏斯特市，离上议院约200码，是英国首都大伦敦地区的警察机关，1829年在内政大臣罗伯特·皮尔主导之下成立。该机构也负担着重大的国家任务，如配合指挥反恐事务、保卫皇室成员及英国政府高官等。

9. **Shropshire:** 什罗浦郡（英格兰西部）。

10. **wash one's dirty linen in public:** 英语习语，意思是家丑外扬。此处把dirty换成clean是想营造幽默效果。

11. **In married life three is company and two is none:** 本意是三人成伴，两人不欢，此处被故意曲解，来表达歪论怪论。

12. **Wilhelm Richard Wagner**（威廉·理查德·瓦格纳，1813年5月22日—1883年2月13日），德国作曲家，著名的古典音乐大师。他是德国歌剧史上一位举足轻重的巨匠，前面承接了莫扎特的歌剧传统，后面开启了后浪漫主义歌剧作曲潮流，理查德·施特劳斯紧随其后。同时，因为他在政治、宗教方面思想的复杂性，成为欧洲音乐史上最具争议的人物。

13. **Belgrave Square:** 贝尔格拉维广场，位于伦敦。

14. **as right as a trivet:** 很健康，一切顺利。

15. **Gorgon:** 戈耳工，希腊神话中的三个长有尖牙，头生毒蛇的蛇发女怪之一。在本段中的意思是可怕的。

四、拓展思考

1. Why or how is *The Importance of Being Earnest* funny? Analyze some aspects of Wilde's wit and the language skills used in the play.

2. Gwendolen's father, Lord Bracknell, never appears in the play, yet Lady Bracknell mentions him often. What picture of his life and marriage do we get from the things Lady Bracknell and Gwendolen say about him?

3. According to the play, what are Wilde's attitudes towards the life of the upper class and modern civilization?

五、延展阅读

王尔德无论作为作家还是社会个体都是极具多重性的。在创作中，一方面，他力主“为艺术而艺术”的创作原则，认为艺术并非是对现实的反映，而是现实模仿艺术，他作品的字里行间无不是对生活的冷嘲热讽；另一方面，尽管他认为艺术创作不受道德的约束，但他的作品如《快乐王子》和《道连·格雷的画像》又表现出明显的道德关怀。在现实生活中，他的社会地位、宗教观和两性观都是充满矛盾的。现今，大众文化中广泛流行的王尔德“毒舌”语录既反映了他对语言的驾驭能力，也反映了他的世俗性。那么，我们应该如何认识和理解王尔德身上的矛盾性和多重性呢?

英国文艺理论家特里·伊格尔顿曾对王尔德的多重性做出过他的解释：“作为一位有着爱尔兰人的他者地位和陷入身份危机的人，王尔德不会被特别烙上传统古典文学的印记，他对这些形式和管理有着强烈的反讽意识。”伊格尔顿如此解读王尔德的写作风格：“王尔德留下了一种嘲讽现实主义的盎格鲁—爱尔兰写作形式，在他嬉笑怒骂、天马行空，疯狂的喜剧下面有着黑色而清醒的亚文化，矛盾和颠覆性的机智里表现出一种深刻的反常规性。”伊格尔顿对王尔德评价的参照意义还可以在本书的第10位和第11位剧作家——卡尔和麦克多纳的作品中得到一定程度的印证。

有兴趣的读者可以阅读伊格尔顿的剧本《圣人王尔德》（*Saint Wilde*，1989）。伊格尔顿是当代著名的英国文艺理论家，出生于爱尔兰。这也是他选择王尔德展开创作的原因。伊格尔顿将该剧授权给了户外日戏剧公司（Filed Day Theatre），一家于1980年成立的爱尔兰戏剧公司。

CHAPTER 3

萧伯纳

George Bernard Shaw

《英国佬的另一个岛》

John Bull's Other Island

一、剧作家简介

萧伯纳（George Bernard Shaw，1856—1950），英国杰出的现实主义戏剧大师、诺贝尔文学奖得主（1925年）。萧伯纳1856年出生于爱尔兰一个没落的贵族家庭。尽管家境并不富裕，但萧伯纳也接受了良好的上等教育。1876年，因父母离异，萧伯纳随母亲迁居伦敦，自此开启了他在伦敦的谋生生涯和创作之路。

在艺术创作上，萧伯纳历经了一段很长的摸索时期。期间，他尝试过写小说和音乐评论，直到他有一次接触到易卜生的戏剧，并深受触动，为此他开始专门研究易卜生的戏剧，并完成了《易卜生主义的精华》一书。在易卜生的影响下，萧伯纳反对“为艺术而艺术”的观点，大力倡导和创作以讨论社会问题为主旨的“新戏剧”。自1892年完成《鳏夫的房产》（*Widowers' Houses*，1892）后，萧伯纳完全找到了自己的声音，相继创作了《华伦夫人的职业》（*Mrs. Warren's Profession*，1893）和《巴巴拉少校》（*Major Barbara*，1905）。在政治上和思想上，萧伯纳是积极的社会活动家和费边社会主义的宣传者。他呼吁对选举制度进行根本的改革，倡导收入平等，主张废除私有财产。萧伯纳一生多产，他的创作黄金期一直延续到20世纪20年代，著名作品有《皮格马利翁》（*Pygmalion*，1912）、《圣女贞德》（*Saint Joan*, 1923）和《苹果车》（*Apple Cart*，1929）等。在语言上，萧伯纳以幽默、讽刺的语言风格见长。

相较于众多西方作家，萧伯纳与中国是特别“亲密”的。萧伯纳曾经于1933年访问中国，与中国文化界诸多名人，如宋庆龄、蔡元培、鲁迅、梅兰芳等有过接触和交流，故中国对于萧伯纳的引介和研究更为深入。

二、剧情简介

《英国佬的另一个岛》（*John Bull's Other Island*，1904）是一部易为中国普通读者所忽略的剧本。不同于萧伯纳以往以伦敦为背景的创作，该剧是以剧作家的家乡——爱尔兰为背景的。本选篇节选自该剧第一幕。

戏剧描述了一名叫作博饶本的英国人在爱尔兰的经历。在这个英国人看来，虽然英国对芬兰、马其顿都负有责任，但对爱尔兰的责任是首要的。博饶本来到爱尔兰，掌握了农场主的地契，勾引当地有财产继承权的女子，进入了议会，并策划使这个地区的经济彻底破产。毋庸置疑，博饶本是典型的英国殖民者的形象代言人。

博饶本的合伙股东杜依尔是英国化的爱尔兰人，他所关心的是他的商业利益——它高于国家和他的同胞的利益。他运用种种诡计迫使小农场主破产以扩大自己的生意。曾当过牧师的克里指责英国掠夺者博饶本和杜依尔之流把爱尔兰这块神圣的土地变成耻辱的地方、变成卖国贼之岛。

该剧一方面以辛辣的语调抨击了野心勃勃的英国佬对被压迫的爱尔兰所实施的皮鞭与甜饼干的伪善政策；另一方面也隐含着剧作家对于自己家乡爱尔兰的困难“哀其不幸、怒其不争”的复杂情感。

三、名篇选读

John Bull's Other Island

ACT I

DOYLE: (*returning*) Where the devil did you pick up that seedy swindler[1]? What was he doing here? (*He goes up to the table where the plans are, and makes a note on one of them, referring to his pocket book as he does so.*)

BROADBENT: There you go! Why are you so down on[2] every Irishman you meet, especially if he's a bit shabby? poor devil! Surely a fellow-countryman may pass you the top of the morning[3] without offence, even if his coat is a bit shiny at the seams.

DOYLE: (*contemptuously*) The top of the morning! Did he call you the broth of a boy[4]? (*He comes to the writing table.*)

BROADBENT: (*triumphantly*) Yes.

DOYLE: And wished you more power to your elbow?

BROADBENT: He did.

DOYLE: And that your shadow might never be less[5]?

BROADBENT: Certainly.

DOYLE: (*taking up the depleted whisky bottle and shaking his head at it*) And he got about half of whisky out of you.

BROADBENT: It did him no harm. He never turned a hair.

DOYLE: How much money did he borrow?

BROADBENT: It was not borrowing exactly. He showed a very honorable spirit about money. I believe he would share his last shilling with a friend.

DOYLE: No doubt he would share his friend's last shilling if his friend was fool enough to let him. How much did he touch you for?

BROADBENT: Oh, nothing. An advance on his salary—for travelling expenses.

DOYLE: Salary! In heaven's name, what for?

BROADBENT: For being my Home Secretary[6], as he very wittily called it.

DOYLE: I don't see the joke.

BROADBENT: You can spoil any joke by being cold blooded about it. I saw it all right when he said it. It was something—something really very amusing about the Home Secretary and the Irish Secretary. At all events, he's evidently the very man to take with me to Ireland to break the ice for me. He can gain the confidence of the people there, and make them friendly to me. Eh? (*He seats himself on the office stool, and tilts it back so that the edge of the standing desk supports his back and prevents his toppling over.*)

DOYLE: A nice introduction, by George! Do you suppose the whole population of Ireland consists of drunken begging letter writers, or that even if it did, they would accept one another as references?

BROADBENT: Pooh! nonsense! He's only an Irishman. Besides, you don't seriously suppose that Haffigan can humbug me, do you?

DOYLE: No; he's too lazy to take the trouble. All he has to do is to sit there and drink your whisky while you humbug yourself. However, we needn't argue about Haffigan, for two reasons. First, with your money in his pocket he will never reach Paddington; there are too many public houses on the way. Second, he's not an Irishman at all.

BROADBENT: Not an Irishman! (*He is so amazed by the statement that he straightens himself and brings the stool bolt upright.*)

DOYLE: Born in Glasgow. Never was in Ireland in his life. I know all about him.

BROADBENT: But he spoke—he behaved just like an Irishman.

DOYLE: Like an Irishman! Man alive; don't you know that all this top-of-the-morning and broth-of-a-boy and more-power-to-your-elbow business is got up in England to fool you, like the Albert Hall[7] concerts of Irish music? No Irishman ever talks like that in Ireland, or ever did, or ever will. But when a thoroughly worthless Irishman comes to England, and finds the whole place full of romantic duffers like you, who will let him loaf and drink and sponge and brag as long as he flatters your sense of moral superiority by playing the fool and degrading himself and his country, he soon learns the antics that take you in. He picks them up at the theatre or the music hall. Haffigan learnt the rudiments from his father, who came from my part of Ireland. I knew his uncles, Matt and Andy Haffigan of Rosscullen.

BROADBENT: (*still incredulous*) But his brogue[8]?

DOYLE: His brogue! A fat lot you know about brogues! I've heard you call a Dublin accent that you could hang your hat on, a brogue[9]. Heaven help you! You don't know the difference between Connemara and Rathmines[10]. (*with violent irritation*) Oh, damn Tim Haffigan! Let's drop the subject; he's not worth wrangling about.

BROADBENT: What's wrong with you today, Larry? Why are you so bitter?

(*Doyle looks at him perplexedly; comes slowly to the writing table; and sits down at the end next the fireplace before replying.*)

DOYLE: Well, your letter completely upset me, for one thing.

BROADBENT: Why?

DOYLE: Your foreclosing this Rosscullen mortgage[11] and turning poor Nick Lestrange out of house and home has rather taken me aback; for I liked the old rascal when I was a boy and has the run of his park to play in. I was brought up on the property.

BROADBENT: But he wouldn't pay the interest. I had to foreclose on behalf of the Syndicate. So now I'm off to Rosscullen to look after the property myself. (*He sits down at the writing table opposite Larry, and adds,* *casually, but with an anxious glance at his partner.*) You're coming with me, of course?

DOYLE: (*rising nervously and recommencing his restless movements*) That's it. That's what I dread. That's what has upset me.

BROADBENT: But don't you want to see your country again after 18 years absence? to see your people, to be in the old home again? To—

DOYLE: (*interrupting him very impatiently*) Yes, yes: I know all that as well as you do.

BROADBENT: Oh well, of course (*with a shrug*) if you take it in that way, I'm sorry.

DOYLE: Never you mind my temper; it's not meant for you, as you ought to know by this time. (*He sits down again, a little ashamed of his petulance; reflects a moment bitterly; then bursts out.*) I have an instinct against going back to Ireland: an instinct so strong that I'd rather go with you to the South Pole than to Rosscullen.

BROADBENT: What! Here you are, belonging to a nation with the strongest patriotism! The most inveterate homing instinct in the world! And you pretend you'd rather go anywhere than back to Ireland. You don't suppose I believe you, do you? In your heart—

DOYLE: Never mind my heart; an Irishman's heart is nothing but his imagination. How many of all those millions that have left Ireland have ever come back or wanted to come back? But what's the use of talking to you? Three verses of twaddle about the Irish emigrant 'sitting on the stile, Mary', or three hours of Irish patriotism in Bermondsey[12] or the Scotland Division of Liverpool, go further with you than all the facts that stare you in the face. Why, man alive, look at me! You know the way I nag, and worry, and carp, and cavil, and disparage, and am never satisfied and never quiet, and try the patience of my best friends.

BROADBENT: Oh, come, Larry! do yourself justice. You're very amusing and agreeable to strangers.

DOYLE: Yes, to strangers. Perhaps if I was a bit stiffer to strangers, and a bit easier at home, like an Englishman, I'd be better company for you.

BROADBENT: We get on well enough. Of course you have the melancholy of the Keltic race—

DOYLE: (*bounding out of his chair*) Good God!

BROADBENT: (*slyly*) —and also its habit of using strong language when there's nothing the matter.

DOYLE: Nothing the matter! When people talk about the Celtic race, I feel as if I could burn down London. That sort of rot does more harm than ten Coercion Acts[13]. Do you suppose a man need be a Celt to feel melancholy in Rosscullen? Why, man, Ireland was people just as England was; and its breed was crossed by just the same invaders[14].

BROADBENT: True. All the capable people in Ireland are of English extraction. It has often struck me as a most remarkable circumstance that the only party in parliament which shows the genuine old English character and spirit is the Irish party[15]. Look at its independence, its determination, its defiance of bad Governments, its sympathy with oppressed nationalities all the world over! How English!

DOYLE: Not to mention the solemnity with which it talks old fashioned nonsense which it knows perfectly well to be a century behind the times. That's English, if you like.

BROADBENT: No, Larry, no. You are thinking of the modern hybrids that now monopolize England. Hypocrites, humbugs, Germans, Jews, Yankees, foreigners, Park Laners, cosmopolitan riffraff[16]. Don't call them English. They don't belong to the dear old island, but to their confounded new empire; and by George! They're worthy of it; and I wish them joy of it.

DOYLE: (*unmoved by this outburst*) There! You feel better now, don't you?

BROADBENT: (*defiantly*) I do. Much better.

DOYLE: My deer Tom, you only need a touch of the Irish climate to be as big a fool as I am myself. If all my Irish blood were poured into your veins, you wouldn't turn a hair of your constitution and character. Go and marry the most English Englishwoman you can find, and then bring up your son in Rosscullen; and that son's character will be so like mine and so unlike yours that everybody will accuse me of being the father. (*with sudden anguish*) Rosscullen! oh, good Lord, Rosscullen! The dullness! The hopelessness! the ignorance! the bigotry!

BROADBENT: (*matter-of-factly*) The usual thing in the country, Larry. Just the same here.

DOYLE: (*hastily*) No, no; the climate is different. Here, if the life is dull, you can be dull too, and no great harm done. (*going off into a passionate dream*) But your wits can't thicken in that soft moist air, on those hillsides of granite rocks and magenta heather. You've no such colors in the sky, no such lure in the distances, no such sadness in the evenings. Oh, the dreaming! the dreaming! The torturing, heart-scalding, never satisfying dreaming, dreaming, dreaming, dreaming! (*Savagely*) No debauchery that ever coarsened and brutalized an Englishman can take the worth and usefulness out of him like that dreaming. An Irishman's imagination never lets him alone, never convinces him, never satisfies him; but it makes him that he can't face reality nor deal with it nor handle it nor conquer it; he can only sneer at them that do, and (*bitterly, at Broadbent*) be 'agreeable to strangers', like a good-for-nothing woman on the streets. (*gabbling at Broadbent across the table*) It's all dreaming, all imagination. He can't be religious. The inspired Churchman that teaches him the sanctity of life and the importance of conduct is sent away empty; while the poor village priest that gives him a miracle or a sentimental story of a saint, has cathedrals built for him out of the pennies of the poor. He can't be intelligently political; he dreams of what the Shan Van Vocht[17] said in ninety-eight. If you want to interest him in Ireland you've got to call the unfortunate island Kathleen ni Hoolihan and pretend she's a little old woman. It saves thinking. It saves working. It saves everything except imagination, imagination, imagination; and imagination's such a torture that you can't bear it without whisky. (*with fierce shivering self-contempt*) At last you get that you can bear nothing real at all; you'd rather starve than cook a meal; you'd rather go shabby and dirty than set your mind to take care of your clothes and wash yourself; you nag and squabble at home because your wife isn't an angel, and she despised you because you're not a hero, and you hate the whole lot round you because they're only poor slovenly useless devils like yourself. (*dropping his voice like a man making some shameful confidence*)

And all the while there goes on a horrible, senseless, mischievous laughter. When you're young, you exchange drinks with other young men, and you exchange vile stories with them, and as you're too futile to be able to help or cheer them, you chaff and sneer and taunt them for not doing the things you aren't do yourself. And all the time you laugh! laugh! laugh! eternal derision, eternal envy, eternal folly, eternal fouling and staining and degrading, until, when you come at last to a country where men take a question seriously and give a serious answer to it, you deride them for having no sense of humor, and plume yourself on your own worthlessness as if it made you better than them.

BROADBENT: (*roused to intense earnestness by DOYLE's eloquence*) Never despair, Larry. There are great possibilities for Ireland. Home Rule will work wonders under English guidance[18].

DOYLE: (*pulled up short, his face twitching with a reluctant smile*) Tom, why do you select my most tragic moments for your most irresistible strokes of humor?

BROADBENT: Humor! I was perfectly serious. What do you mean? Do you doubt my seriousness about Home Rule?

DOYLE: I am sure you are serious, Tom, about the English guidance.

BROADBENT: (*quiet reassured*) Of course I am. Our guidance is the important thing. We English must place our capacity for government without stint at the service of nations who are less fortunately endowed in that respect; so as to allow them to develop in perfect freedom to the English level of self-government, you know. You understand me?

DOYLE: Perfectly. And Rosscullen will understand you too.

BROADBENT: (*cheerfully*) Of course it will. So that's all right. (*He pulls up his chair and settles himself comfortably to lecture DOYLE.*) Now Larry, I've listened carefully to all you've said about Ireland, and I can see nothing whatever to prevent your coming with me. What does it all come to? Simply that you were only a young fellow when you were in Ireland. You'll find all that chaffing and drinking and not knowing what to be at in Peckham just the same as in Donnybrook. You looked at Ireland with a boy's eyes and saw only boyish things. Come back with me and look at it with a man's, and get a better opinion of your country.

DOYLE: I dare say you're partly right in that, at all events I know very well that if I had been the son of a laborer instead of the son of a country landagent, I should have struck more grit than I did. Unfortunately I'm not going back to visit the Irish nation, but to visit my father and Aunt Judy and Nora Reilly and Father Dempsey and the rest of them.

BROADBENT: Well, why not? They'll be delighted to see you, now that England has made a man of you.

DOYLE: (*struck by this*) Ah! You hit the mark there, Tom, with true British inspiration.

BROADBENT: Common sense, you mean.

DOYLE: (*quickly*) No, I don't; you've no more common sense than a gander. No Englishman has any common sense, or ever had, or ever will have. You're going on a sentimental expedition for perfectly ridiculous reasons with your head full of political nonsense that would not take in the eye with the simple truth about myself and my father.

BROADBENT: (*amazed*) I never mentioned your father.

DOYLE: (*not heeding the interruption*) There he is in Rosscullen, a landagent who's always been in a small way because he's a Catholic, and the landlords are mostly Protestants. What with land courts reducing rents and Land Purchase Acts turning big estates into little holdings[19], he'd be a beggar if he hadn't taken to collecting the new purchase instalments instead of the old rents. I doubt if he's been further from home than Athenmullet for twenty years. And here am I, made a man of, as you say, by England.

BROADBENT: (*apologetically*) I assure you I never meant—

DOYLE: Oh, don't apologize; it's quite true. I daresay I've learnt something in America and a few other remote and inferior spots; but in the main it is by living with you and working in double harness with you that I have learnt to live in a real world and not in an imaginary one. I owe more to you than to any Irishman.

BROADBENT: (*shaking his head with a twinkle in his eye*) Very friendly of you, Larry, old man, but all blarney. I like blarney; but it's rot, all the same.

DOYLE: No, it's not. I should never have done anything without you; though I never stop wondering at that blessed old head of yours with all its ideas in watertight compartments, and all the compartments warranted impervious to anything it doesn't suit you to understand.

BROADBENT: (*invincible*) Unmitigated rot, Larry, I assure you.

DOYLE: Well, at any rate you will admit that all my friends are either Englishmen or men of the big world that belongs to the big Powers. All the serious part of my life has been lived in that atmosphere; all the serious part of my work has been done with men of that sort. Just think of me as I am now going back to Rosscullen! to that hell of littleness and monotony! How am I to get on with a little country landagent that ekes out his 5 percent with a little farming an a scrap of house property in the nearest country town? What am I to say to him? What is he to say to me?

BROADBENT: (*scandalized*) But you're father and son, man!

DOYLE: What difference does that make? What would you say if I proposed a visit to your father?

BROADBENT: (*with filial rectitude*) I always made a point if going to see my father regularly until his mind gave way.

DOYLE: (*concerned*) Has he gone mad? You never told me.

BROADBENT: He has joined the Tariff Reform League[20]. He would never have done that if his mind had not been weakened. (*beginning to declaim*) He has fallen a victim to the arts of a political charlatan who—

DOYLE: (*interrupting him*) You mean that you keep clear of your father because he differs from you about Free Trade, and you don't want to quarrel with him. Well, think of me and my father! He's a Nationalist an a Separatist[21]. I'm a metallurgical chemist turned civil engineer. Now whatever else metallurgical chemistry may be, it's not national. It's international. And my business and yours as civil engineers is to join countries, not to separate them. The one real political conviction that our business has rubbed into us is that frontiers are hindrances and flags confounded nuisances.

注释

1. **seedy swindler:** 破破烂烂的骗子。（指Tim Haffigan）
2. **be down on sb.:** 对某人有怨气。
3. **the top of the morning:** 爱尔兰人早上打招呼的用语。
4. **the broth of a boy:** 棒小伙子（爱尔兰说法）。
5. **your shadow might never be less:** 祝你长生不老永葆青春（爱尔兰说法）。
6. **my Home Secretary:** 我的内政大臣。
7. **Albert Hall:** Royal Albert Hall 位于伦敦，是世界著名演出场所。
8. **brogue:** 土腔（指爱尔兰口音的英语）。
9. 这句话的意思是：有一次我听见你把很重的都柏林音叫作爱尔兰土腔。都柏林是爱尔兰首都，都柏林音不是爱尔兰土腔。杜依尔这样说是在讽刺博饶本不懂爱尔兰土腔。
10. **Connemara and Rathmines:** 这两个地方分别在爱尔兰的极东部和极西部。这句话的意思是博饶本连爱尔兰的东部西部都分不清。
11. **Your foreclosing this Rosscullen mortgage:** 取消罗斯库伦田庄的赎典权。罗斯库伦是本剧的主要场所，是经济落后的爱尔兰农村。土地原先在像尼克·莱斯特兰奇（Nick Lestrange）这样的大地主手里，由于他们被英国压榨，加上生产方式落后，大半破产了，于是把土地典押给英国资本家。结果英国资本家开始“土地开拓”，经营工商业，使农民放弃农业，另找出路，有的农民就沦为企业中的奴隶。本剧所描述的就是这种转变过程。
12. **Bermondsey:** 柏孟塞（地名，位于伦敦南部）。
13. that sort of rot does more harm than ten Coercion Acts的意思是这一类废话比十个“强制法令”还要坏。（“强制法令”是英国政府剥夺爱尔兰人自由，并用强制手段统治爱尔兰的法令）
14. 英伦三岛在中世纪的前半期遭到北欧民族的侵略，这些外来民族中有些定居下来与土著民族通婚。
15. **the Irish Party:** 爱尔兰党也称爱尔兰议会党（Irish Parliamentary Party），通常是用来表示爱尔兰民族主义力量在英国议会中的代表。实现爱尔兰“自治”和在爱尔兰都柏林建立分离的爱尔兰议会是该党为之奋斗的目标。
16. **You are thinking of the modern hybrids that now monopolize... cosmo politan riffraff:** 这里指的是现在霸占着英国那些混血种的新牌英国人。这批人都是伪君子、骗子、德国人、美国人、公园路的住户（公园路为伦敦街道，以高档酒店及住宅而闻名），还有那些没有国籍在世界上东飘西荡的人。
17. **He can't be intelligently political; he dreams of what the Shan Van Vocht said in ninety-eight.** 这句话的意思是：在政治上爱尔兰人也是个糊涂虫，他还梦想着“老妇人”在1798年所说的话。[Shan Van Vocht是盖尔语，意思是“老妇人”，也是下文所说

的霍利汉之女凯瑟琳。她所说的是“爱尔兰人在1798年的主张”。1798年，爱尔兰人举行了大起义，他们希望在法国军队的帮助下，反抗英国殖民军，但失败了。诗人叶芝写过一个剧本《胡里痕的凯瑟琳》（*Cathleen ni Houlihan*，1902）讲的就是这个故事：一个老妇人来到一个村落，人们问她为何流落他乡，她说有人把她的四块土地抢走了。剧中的老妇人象征着爱尔兰，四块土地就是爱尔兰的四个省。]

18. **Home Rule will work wonders under English guidance:** 英国人领导下的自治会创造奇迹。

19. **Land Purchase Acts turning big estates into little holdings:** 地产购买法令把大庄业分成许多小庄业。

20. 自由党主张贸易自由，保守党主张关税保护，通过关税限制进口货物来保护本国货物的生产不被外国货物排挤。博饶本是自由党，他的父亲加入关税改良协会，显然是保守党，所以两人不和。

21. 分裂主义者主张爱尔兰脱离英国的统治而独立。

四、拓展思考

1. Why is the play entitled as *John Bull's Other Island*? What's the origin and connotation of John Bull?

2. Shaw, along with such predecessors as Jonathan Swift, Richard Sheridan and Oscar Wilde, was labelled as Anglo-Irish writers, who showed complicated feelings to their motherland. How do you understand the satire in this play?

3. Please go further for background knowledge and state the relationship between England and Ireland since the 16th century.

五、延展阅读

萧伯纳虽然出生于爱尔兰，也活跃于爱尔兰文艺复兴时期，但他并没有参加爱尔兰的戏剧运动，与爱尔兰剧作家们的关系也是若即若离，因此很多读者认为萧伯纳是典型的英国作家。《英国佬的另一个岛》是萧伯纳应叶芝之邀为阿贝剧院专门创作的。该剧最能体现萧伯纳创作中的爱尔兰关怀意识。

“约翰·布尔”是苏格兰讽刺作家阿巴恩诺特（John Arbuthnot，1667—1735）的小说《约翰·布尔的身世》（*History of John Bull*，1712）中的一位好战人物，他代表英国。“另一个岛”是他所吹嘘的、有异议的爱尔兰。这种利用用典和反讽是萧伯纳一贯的创作风格，一如他在《皮格玛利翁》中的标题借用古希腊故事造成反讽效果一样。

然而，本剧并非一味批评英国对于爱尔兰的政治欺骗和经济掠夺。萧伯纳对同乡爱尔兰人的性格弱点——爱辩论和不踏实的空想主义也同样进行了挖苦和讽刺。正是因为该剧无法呈现“真实”的爱尔兰形象，只是延续了英国戏剧舞台上一贯被歪曲的爱尔兰人，并完全与叶芝在20世纪初所倡导的“重建爱尔兰人形象”的文化理念相冲突，因此，本剧曾经被以叶芝为代表的阿贝剧院的剧作人退稿。

这一剧本背后的故事可以引发读者更深入地考察20世纪爱尔兰戏剧运动民族化的时代意义与时代局限，更深刻地领会萧伯纳在当代爱尔兰文学研究中被重新审视和挖掘爱尔兰性的文化价值。

CHAPTER 4

尤金·奥尼尔

Eugene O'Neil

《诗人的气质》

A Touch of The Poet

一、剧作家简介

尤金·奥尼尔（*Eugene O'Neill*，1888—1953）出生在纽约百老汇的一家旅馆里，父亲詹姆斯·奥尼尔是一位著名演员，并对他走上戏剧创作之路影响至深。1906年，奥尼尔进入普林斯顿大学学习，但他中途退学了。之后，奥尼尔远航去了南美和南非，他与生活在社会底层的人交友，充分体验了生活的艰辛，为其日后的写作提供了充足的准备。1916年，奥尼尔的独幕剧《东航卡迪夫》（*Bound East for Cardiff*）第一次被搬上了舞台，这既标志着奥尼尔创作生涯的开始，也昭示着美国戏剧时代的到来。

1920年，奥尼尔的作品《天外边》（*Beyond the Horizon*，*1920*）引来一片如潮的好评。此后的十四年里，奥尼尔的作品一直在百老汇上演，例如《毛猿》（*The Hairy Ape*，1922）、《榆树下的欲望》（*Desire under the Elms*，1924）、《无穷的岁月》（*Days without Ends*，1934）等。然而在此后的1934年到1946年之间，奥尼尔因患病进入了短暂的沉寂，但是他却一直在酝酿新的作品。终于，奥尼尔在1946带着他的新作 《送冰的人来了》（*The Iceman Cometh*，1946）重回百老汇，也开启了他最后也是最卓越的创作阶段。这一阶段，奥尼尔的主要作品包括《长夜漫漫》（*Long Day is Journey into the Night*，1956）、《月照不幸人》（*A Moon for the Misbegotten*，1957）以及《诗人的气质》（*A Touch of the Poet*，1958）。奥尼尔曾四次获得普利策奖，并于1936年获得诺贝尔文学奖。

奥尼尔一生坚持不懈地革新戏剧艺术。他把戏剧从19世纪的传统束缚中解放出来，使之在现实生活中扎根、成长。他首次把现实主义乃至自然主义的传统手法运用于戏剧创作中，他的艺术风格以多样和精深圆熟而著称。他博览群书，深谙欧洲戏剧传统，且深受易卜生、尼采和弗洛伊德的影响。同时，奥尼尔还广泛地借鉴现代文学艺术的表现手法譬如意识流，这使得他的作品成功地揭示出现代人感情和心理的复杂性。奥尼尔永不止步的戏剧尝试丰富了美国戏剧，并影响到后来的剧作家。可以说，奥尼尔将会被视为美国的莎士比亚而载入美国戏剧的史册。

二、剧情简介

《诗人的气质》主要围绕爱尔兰移民科尼利厄斯·梅洛迪一家展开。梅洛迪出生在爱尔兰城堡，曾是惠灵顿公爵手下一位善战的少校军官，因对一位女士的不检点行为而失去了军职，来到新英格兰地区一个荒凉的小镇上开酒馆谋生。梅洛迪对过去的荣誉念念不忘，表面上经常摆出一副欧洲绅士派头，佯装依然过着“奢华”的生活，但内心十分孤寂，无法寻找到真我，也无法获得“美国佬”的认同，只有每天借酒浇愁，经常对着镜子孤芳自赏，背诵英国大诗人拜伦的诗句。梅洛迪因不满哈福德家对女儿萨拉与其儿子西蒙婚姻的态度，决定和他的老部下克里根一起去找哈福德要求其道歉或决斗，但结果他不仅没有见到老哈福德，还被他家的仆人和警察毒打了一顿。“美国佬”的一顿毒打使梅洛迪头脑清醒起来。他埋葬了自己之前引以为傲的红色军服，开枪打死了自己心爱的骏马。他也不再冒充绅士，而是自愿与自己以前瞧不起的爱尔兰穷乡们不摆任何架子地喝酒，并且迅速改变了自己的政治立场。

三、名篇选读

A Touch of The Poet

ACT Ⅳ

SARA: What a fool I was to be afraid! I might know you'd never do it as long as a drink of whiskey was left in the world! So it was the mare you shot? (*She bursts into uncontrollable, hysterical laughter.*) It penetrates Melody's stupor and he stiffens rigidly on his chair, but his legs remain fixed on the table top.

NORA: Sara! Stop! For the love av[1] God, how can you laugh—!

SARA: I can't help it, Mother. Didn't you hear Jamie? It was the mare he shot! (*She gives way to laughter again.*)

NORA: (*distractedly*) Stop it! I'm sayin'! (*SARA puts her hand over her mouth to shut off the sound of her laughing, but her shoulders still shake. Nora sinks* *on the chair at rear of the table. She mutters dazedly.*) Kilt his beautiful mare? He must be mad entirely.

MELODY: (*suddenly speaks, without looking up, in the broadest brogue, his voice coarse and harsh*) I ave[2] Sara laugh. Sure, who could blame her? I am roarin meself inside me. It's the damnedest joke a man ivir played on himself since time began. (*They stare at him. SARA's laughter stops. She is startled and repelled by his brogue. Then she stares at him suspiciously; her face hardening.*)

SARA: What a joke? Do you think murdering the poor make a good joke? (*MELODY stiffens for a second, but that is all. He doesn't look up or reply.*)

NORA: (frightened) Look at the dead face on him, Sara. He is like a corpse. (*She reaches out and touches one of his hands on the table top with a furtive tenderness-pleadingly.*) Con, darlin'. Don't!

MELODY: (*looks up at her. His expression changes so that his face loses all its remaining distinction and appears vulgar and common, with a loose, leering grin on his swollen lips.*) Let you not worry. Allanah. Sure, I am no corpse, and with a few drinks in me, I'll soon be lively enough to suit you.

NORA: (*miserably confused*) Will you listen to him. Sara, puttin' on the brogue to torment us.

SARA: (*growing more uneasy but sneering*) Pay no heed to him, Mother. He's play acting to amuse himself. If he is that cruel and shameless after what he's done—

NORA: (*defensively*) No, it's the blow on the head he got fightin' the police.

MELODY: (*vulgarly*) The blow, me foot! That's Jamie Cregan's blather. Sure, it'd take more than a few clubs on the head to darken my wits long. Me brains, if I have any, is clear as a bell. And I am not puttin' on brogue to tormint you, me darlint. Nor play-actin', Sara. That was the major's game. It's quare, surely, for the two av ye to object when I talk in me natural tongue, and yours, and don't put on airs like the late lamented auld liar and lunatic, Major Cornelius Melody, av His Majesty's Seventh Dragoons, used to do.

NORA: God save us, Sara, will you listen!

MELODY: But he's dead now, and his last bit av lyin' pride is murthered and stinkin'. (*He pats NORA's hand with what seems to be genuine comforting affection.*) So let you be aisy, darlint. He'll nivir again hurt you with his sneers, and his pretindin' he's a gintleman, blatherin' about pride and honor, and his showin' off before the Yankees[3], and thim laughin' at him, prancing around drunk on his beautiful thoroughbred mare— (*He gulps as if he were choking back a sob.*) For she's dead, too, poor baste.

SARA: (*This is becoming unbearable for her—tensely.*) Why did you kill her?

MELODY: Why did the major, you mean! Be Christ, you are stupider that I thought you, if you can't see that. Wasn't she the livin' reminder, so to spake, av all his lyin' boasts and dreams? He meant to kill her first wid one pistol, and then himself wid the other. But Frix, he saw the shot that killed her had finished him, too. There wasn't much pride left in the auld lunatic, anyway, and seeing her die made an end av him. So he didn't bother shooting himself, because it'd be a mad thing to waste a good bullet on a corpse! (*He laughs coarsely.*)

SARA: (*tensely*) Father! Stop it!

MELODY: Didn't I tell you there was a great joke in it? Well, that's the joke. (*He begins to laugh again but he chokes on a stifled sob. Suddenly his face loses the coarse, leering, brutal expression and is full of anguished grief. He speaks without brogue, not to them but aloud to himself.*) Blessed Christ, the look in her eyes by the lantern light with life ebbing out of them wondering and sad, but still trustful, not reproaching me—with no fear in them—proud, understanding pride—loving me—she saw I was dying with her. She understood! She forgave me! (*He stars to sob but wrenches himself out of it and speaks in broad, jeering brogue.*) Begorra, if that wasn't the mad Major's ghost speakin'! But he damned to him, he won't haunt me long, if I know it! I intend to live at me case form now and not let the dead bother me, but enjoy life in my proper station as auld Nick Melody's son. I'll bury his Major's damned red livery av bloody England deep in the ground and he can haunt its grave if he likes, and boast to the lonely night ave Talavera and the ladies of Spain and fightin' the French! (*with a leer*) Troth, I think the boy is right when they saw he stole the uniform and the nivir fought under

Wellington[4] at all. He was a terrible liar, as I remember him.

NORA: Con, darlin', don't be grievin' about the mare. Sure, you can get another. I'll manage—

SARA: Mother! Hush! (*to Melody, furiously*) Father, will you stop this mad game you're playing—!

MELODY: (*roughly*) Game, is it? You'll find it's no game. It was the major played a game all his life, the crazy auld loon, and the cheated only himself. But I'll be contend to stay meself in the proper station I was born to, form this day on. (*with a cunning leer at SARA*). And it's meself feels it me dury to give you a bit av fatherly advice. Sara, darlint, while my mind is on it. I know you've great ambition, so remember it's to hell wid honor if ye want to rise in this world. Remember the blood in your veins and be your grandfather's true descendent. There was an able man for you! Be Jaysus, he nivir felt anything beneath him that could gain him something, and for lyin' tricks to swindle the bloody fools of gintry. There wasn't his match in Ireland, and he ended up wid a grand estate, and a castle, and a pile av gold in the bank.

SARA: (*distractedly*) Oh, I hate you!

NORA: Sara!

MELODY: (*goes on as if he hadn't heard*) I know he'd advise that to give you a first step up. darlint, you must make the young Yankee ginteman have you in his bed, and afher he's had you, weep great tears and appeal to his honor to marry you and save yours. Be God, he'll nivir resist that, if I know him, for he is a young fool, full av decency and dreams, and looney, too, wid a touch av the poet in him. Oh, it'll be aisy for you—

SARA: (*goaded beyond bearing*) I'll make you stop your dirty brogue and your play-acting! (*She leans toward him and speaks with taunting vindictiveness, in brogue herself.*) Thanks you kindly but I've already taken your wise advice, Father. I made him have me in his bed, while you was out drunk fightin' the police.

NORA: (*frightenedly*) Sara! Hault your brazen tongue!

MELODY: (*His body stiffens on his chair and the coarse leer vanishes from his face. It becomes his old face. His eyes fix on her in a threatening stare. He speaks* *slowly, with difficulty keeping his words in brogue.*) Did you now, God bless you! I might have known you'd mot take any chance that the auld loon av a Major, going out to revenge an insult to you, would spoil your schemes. (*He forces a horrible grin.*) Be the living God, it's me should be proud this night that one av the Yankee gintry has stooped to be seduced by my slut av a daughter! (*Still keeping his eyes fixed on hers, he begins to rise from his chair, his right hand groping along the table top until it clutches the dueling pistol. He aims it at Sara's heart, like an automaton, his eyes as cold, deadly, and merciless as they must have been in his duels of long ago. SARA is terrified but she stands unflinchingly.*)

NORA: (*horror-stricken, lunges from her chair and grabs his arm*) Con! For the love av God! Would you be murthering Sara? (*A dazed look comes over his face. He grows limp and sinks back on his chair and lets the pistol slide from his fingers on the table. He draws a shuddering breath—then laughs hoarsely.*)

MELODY: (*with a coarse leer*) Murtherin' Sara, is it? Are ye daft, Nora? Sure, all I want is to congratulate her!

SARA: (*hopelessly*) Oh! (*She sinks down on her chair at rear of the center table and covers her face with her hands.*)

NORA: (*with pitifully well-meant reassurance*) It's all right, Con. The young lad wants to marry her as soon as can be, she told me, and he did before.

MELODY: Musha, but that's kind of him! Be God, we ought to be proud av our daughter, Nora. Lave it to her to get what she wants by hook or crook. And won't we be proud watchin' her rise in the world till she's a grand lady!

NORA: (*simply*) We will, surely.

SARA: Mother!

MELODY: She'll have some trouble, rootin' out his dreams. He's set in his proud, noble ways, but she'll find the right trick! I'd lay a pound, if I had one, to a shilling she'll see the day when she'll wear fine silks and drive in a carriage wid a naygur coachman behind spankin' thorough breds, her nose in the air; and she'll live in a Yankee mansion, as big as a castle, on a grand estate av stately woodland and soft green meadows and a lake. (*with a leering chuckle*) Be the Saints, I'll start her on her way to making her a wedding present av the Major's place where he let her young gintleman build his cabin—the land the Yankees swindled him into buyin' for his American estate, the mad fool! (*He glances at the dueling pistol—jeeringly.*) Speakin' av the departed, may his soul roast in hell, what am I doin' wid his pistol? Be God, I don't need pistols. Me fists, or a club if it's handy, is cnough. Didn't me and Jamie lick a whole regiment av police this night?

NORA: (*stoutly*) You did, and if there wasn't so many av thim—

MELODY: (*turns to her—grinningly*) That's the talk, darlint! Sure, there's devil a more loyal wife in the whole world— (*be pauses, staring at her—then suddenly kisses her on the lips, roughly but with a strange real tenderness*) and I love you.

NORA: (*with amazed, unthinking joy*) Oh, Con!

MELODY: (*grinning again*) I've meant to tell you often, only the Major, damn him, has me under his proud thumb. (*He pulls her over and kisses her hair.*)

NORA: Is it kissin' my hair—!

MELODY: I am. Why wouldn't I? You have beautiful hair, God bless you! And don't remember what the Major used to tell you. The gintleman's sneers he put on is buried with him. I'll be a real husband to you, and help ye run this shebeen, instead of being a sponge. I'll fire Mickey and tend the bar myself, like any father's son ought to.

NORA: You'll not! I'll nivir let you!

MELODY: (*leering cunningly*) Well, I offered, remember. It's you refused. Sure. I'm not in love with work, I'll confess, and maybe you're right not to trust me too near the whiskey. (*He licks his lips.*) Be Jaysus, that reminds me. I've not had a taste for hours. I'm dyin' av thirst.

NORA: (stars to rise) I'll get you—

MELODY: (*pushes her back on his chair*) Ye'll not. I want company and singin' and dancin' and great laughter. I'll join the boys in the bar and help Cousin Jamie celebrate our wonderful shindy wid the police. (*He gets* *up. His old soldierly bearing is gone. His slouches and his movements are shambling and dumpy; his big hairy hands dangling at his side. In his torn, disheveled, dirt-stained uniform, he looks like a loutish, grinning down.)*

NORA: You ought to go to bed, Con darlin', with your head burted.

MELODY: Me head? Faix, it was nivir so clear while the Major lived to torment me, makin' me tell and lies to excuse his devilments, (*He grins.*) and I ain't tired a bit. I am fresh as a man new born. So I'll say goodnight to you, darlint. (*He bends and kisses her. SARA has lifted her tear-stained face from her hands and is staring at him with a strange, anguished look of desperation. He leers at her.*) And you go to bed, too, Sara. Torth, you deserve a long, dreamless slape after you've accomplished this day.

SARA: (*springs to her feet*) Father! Don't go in with those drunken scum! Don't let them hear and see you! You can drink all you like here. Jamie will come and keep you company. He'll laugh and sing and help you celebrate Talavera[5]—

MELODY: (*roughly*) To hell wid Talavera! (*His eyes are fastened on the mirror. He leers into it.*) Be Jaysus, if it ain't the mirror the auld loon was always admirin' his mug in while he spouted Byron to pretend himself was a lord wid a touch av the poet— (*He strikes a pose which is a vulgar burlesque o his old before-the-mirror one and recites in mocking brogue.*)

"I have not loved the World, nor the World me;
I have not flatthered uts rank breath, nor bowed
To uts idolatries a pashunt knee,
Nor coined me cheek to smiles, —nor cried aloud
In worship av an echo: in the crowd
They couldn't deem me one av such—I stood
Among thim, but not av thim—[6]"

(*He guffaws contemptuously.*) Be Christ, if he wasn't the joke av the world, the Major. He should have been a clown in a circus. God rest his soul in the flames av torment. (*roughly*) But to hell wid the dead. (*The noise in the bar rises to an uproar of laughter as if Jamie has just made some climactic point in his story. Melody looks away from the mirror to the bar door.*) Be God, I'm alive and in the crowd they can deem me one av such! I'll be among thim and av thim, too—and make up for the lonely dog's life the Major led me. (*He goes to the bar door.*)

SARA: (*starts toward him—beseechingly*) Father! Don't put this final shame on yourself. You're not drunk now. There's no excuse you can give yourself. You'll be as dead to yourself after. As if you'd shot yourself along with the mare!

MELODY: (*leering with a wink at Nora*) Listen to her, Nora, reproachin' me because I'm not drunk. Troth, that's a condition soon mended. (*He puts his hand on the knob of the door.*)

SARA: Father!

NORA: (*has given way to such complete physical exhaustion, she hardly hears, much less comprehends what is said—dully*) Lave him alone, Sara. It's best.

MELODY: (*as another roar is heard from the bar*) I'm missin' a lot av fun. Be God, I've a bit of news to tell the boys that'll make them roar the house down. The Major's passin' to his eternal rest has set me free to jine the Democrats, and I'll vote for Andy Jackson[7], the friend av the common men like me, God bless him. (*He grins with anticipation.*) Wait till the boys hear that! (He starts to turn the knob.)

SARA: (*rushes to him and grabs his arm*) No! I won't let you! It's my pride. Too. (*She stammers.*) Listen! Forgive me, Father! I know it's my fault—always sneering and insulting you—but I only meant the lies in it. The truth—Talavera—the Duke praising your bravery—an officer in his army—even the ladies in Spain—deep down that's been my pride, too—that I was your daughter. So don't—I'll do anything you ask—I'll even tell Simon—that after his father's insult to you—I'm too proud to marry a Yankee coward's son!

MELODY: (*has been visible crumbling as he listens until he appears to have no character left in which to hide and defend himself. He cries wildly and despairingly, as if he saw his last hope of escape suddenly cut off.*) Sara! For the love of God, stop—let me go—!

NORA: (*dully*) Lave your poor father be. It's best. (*In a flash melody recovers* *and is the leering peasant again.*)

SARA: (*with bitter hopelessness*) Oh, Mother! Why couldn't you be still!

MELODY: (*roughly*) Why can't you, ye mean. I warned ye what ye'd get if ye kept on interferin' and tryin' to raise the dead. (*He cuffs her on the side of the bead. It is more of a playful push that a blow, but it knocks her off balance back to the end of the table at center.*)

NORA: (*aroused—bewilderedly*) God forgive you. Con! (*angrily*) Don't you be hittin' Sara now. I've put up with a lot but I won't—

MELODY: (*with rough good nature*) Shut up, darlint. I won't have to again. (He grins leeringly at Sara.) That'll teach you, me proud Sara! I know you won't try raisin' the dead any more. And let me hear no more gab out of you about not marryin' the young lad upstairs. Be Jaysus, haven't ye any honor? Ye seduced him and ye'll make an honest gentleman av him if I have to march ye both by the scruff av the neck to the nearest church. (*He chuckles, then leeringly.*) And now with you permission, ladies both, I'll join me good friends in the bar. (*He opens the door and passes into the bar, closing the door behind him. There is a roar of welcoming drunken shouts, pounding of glasses on bar and tables, then quiet as if he had raised a hand for silence, followed by his voice greeting them and ordering drinks, and other roars of acclaim mingled with the music of RILEY's pipes. SARA remains standing by the side of the center table, her shoulders bowed, her head hanging, staring at the floor.*)

NORA: (*overcome by physical exhaustion again, sighs*) Don't mind his giving you a slap. He's still quare in his head. But he'll sing and laugh and drink a power av whiskey and slape sound after, and tomorrow he'll be himself again—maybe.

SARA: (*dully, aloud to herself rather than to her mother*) No. He'll never be. He's beaten at last and he wants to stay beaten. Well, I did my best. Though why I did, I don't know. I must have his crazy pride in me. (*She lifts her head, her face burdening—bitterly.*) I mean, the late Major Melody's pride. I mean, I did have it. Now it's dead—thank God—and I'll make a better wife for Simon. (*There is a sudden bull in the noise from the bar, as if someone had called for silence—then Melody's voice is plainly heard* *in the silence as he shouts a toast: "Here's to out next President, Andy Jackson! Hurroo for Auld Hickory*[8]*, God bless him!" There is drunken chorus of answering "hurroos" that shakes the walls.*)

NORA: Glory be to God, cheerin' for Andy Jackson! Did you hear him, Sara?

SARA: (*her face hard*) I heard someone. But it wasn't any one I ever knew of want to know.

NORA: (*as if she hadn't heard*) Ah, well, that' s good. They won't all be hatin' him now. (*She pauses—her tired, worn face becomes suddenly shy and tender.*) Did you hear him tellin' me he loved me, Sara? Did you see him kiss me on the mouth—and then kiss my hari? (*She gives a little, soft laugh.*) Sure, he must have gone mad altogether!

SARA: (*stares at her mother. Her face softens.*) No, Mother, I know he meant it. He'll keep on meaning it, too. Mother. He'll be free to, now. (*She smile strangely.*) Maybe I deserved the slap for interfering.

NORA: (*preoccupies with her own thoughts*) And if he wants to kape on makin' game of everyone, puttin' on the brogue and actin' like one av thim in there—(*She nods toward the bar.*) Well, why shouldn't he if it brings him peace and company in his loneliness? God pity him, he's had to live all his life alone in the hell av pride. (*proudly*) And I'll play any game he likes and give him love in it. Haven't I always? (*She smiles.*) Sure, I have no pride at all—except that.

SARA: (*stares at her—moved*) You're a strange, noble woman, Mother. I'll try and be like you. (*She comes over and hugs her—then she smiles tenderly.*) I'll wager Simon never heard the shot or anything. He was sleeping like a baby when I left him. A cannon wouldn't wake him. (*In the bar, RILEY starts playing a reel on his pipes and ther is the stamp of dancing feet. For a moment Sara's face becomes hard and bitter again. She tries to be mocking.*) Faith, Patch Riley don't know it but he's playing a requiem for the dead. (*Her voice trembles.*) May the hero of Talavera rest in peace! (*She breaks down and sobs, hiding her face on her mother's shoulder—bewilderedly.*) But why should I cry, Mother? Why do I mourn for him?

NORA: (*at once forgetting her own exhaustion, is all tender, loving help and* *comfort*) Don't, darlin', don't. You're destroyed with tiredness, that's all. Come on to bed, now, and I'll help you undress and tuck you in. (*trying to rouse her—in a teasing tone*) Shame on you to cry when you have love. What would the young lad thinks of you?

注释

1. **av:** 爱尔兰土腔,指英语单词of。
2. **ave:** 爱尔兰土腔，指英语单词have；下一行中的ivir指英语单词never。后面的台词中还有很多爱尔兰土腔词汇，一般根据上下文都能猜到它们的意思。
3. **Yankees:** “扬基人”这个词在美国有两层意思。用于美国国外，它泛指一切美国人；用于美国国内，它指的是新英格兰和北部一些州的美国人。
4. **Wellington:** 威灵顿，别名铁公爵，拿破仑战争时期的英军将领，第21位英国首相，最初于印度军中发迹，西班牙半岛战争（1808—1814）时期建立战功，并在打败拿破仑的滑铁卢战役（1815）中分享胜利。
5. **Talavera:** 原指西班牙一个市镇，此处指塔拉维拉之战。
6. 出自拜伦的长诗《恰尔德哈洛尔德游记》第四章，第184节。这个诗节译成中文的意思是：

   我没有爱过这人世，人世也不爱我；

   它的臭恶气息，我从来也不赞美；

   没有强露欢颜去奉承，不随声附和；

   也未曾向它偶像崇拜的教条下跪；

   因此世人也无法把我当作同类；

   我侧身其中，却不是他们中的一个……（杨熙龄译）
7. **Andy Jackson:** 安德鲁·杰克逊（1767—1845），第七任美国总统（1829—1837）、首任佛罗里达州州长、新奥尔良战役战争英雄、民主党创建者之一，杰克逊式民主因他而得名。在美国政治史上，19世纪20年代与30年代的第二党体系（Second Party System）以他为极端的象征。因做法强硬而知名的杰克逊，绰号“老山胡桃”（Old Hickory）及“印第安人杀手”，是首位出于与美国边陲地带的总统（他出生于南卡罗来那州，但大多时候居于田纳西州）。
8. **Auld Hickory:** 安德鲁·杰克逊总统的绰号——老山胡桃。

四、拓展思考

1. In the play, Cornelius Melody always recites Byron's poetry, both in American tone and Irish tone. What does the poem tell us? Why does Melody always recite the poem? What is the connotation of "a touch of the poet"?
2. Every time Sara speaks with Irish accent, Cornelius Melody would despise Sara and make her correct her "vulgar" behavior. But after his battle with Mr. Harford, he himself adopts the Irish accent. Why does this change happen?
3. Eugene O'Neil devotes all his life to American drama's innovation, and he is a master of expressionism. Analyze some expressionism ways O'Neil uses in the play.

五、延展阅读

不同于奥尼尔的代表作如《长夜漫漫》《毛猿》等，《诗人的气质》十分清晰地展露了剧作家的爱尔兰裔身份。或许是因为爱尔兰裔的身份和家庭熏染，奥尼尔才得以如此轻松而娴熟地驾驭并刻画爱尔兰人的形象和身份意识。近年来，国内外针对奥尼尔的研究开始关注剧作家作品中的爱尔兰性，这同对盎格鲁—爱尔兰作家（如斯威夫特、谢里丹、王尔德、萧伯纳和贝克特等）的研究如出一辙，展现了学界研究的新突破和新动态。

17世纪以来，爱尔兰、英国和美国三国之间的国族关系变得复杂且紧密起来。17世纪，英国爆发资产阶级革命（又称清教革命），大量的英国清教徒不堪政治迫害漂洋过海，到达美国。与此同时，英国采用武力彻底改变对爱尔兰岛的殖民方式。克伦威尔率军登岛后，对岛上的天主教徒所在村庄进行灭绝式的杀戮，导致很多爱尔兰人纷纷逃离至欧洲大陆或美洲，埋下了几个世纪爱尔兰天主教与英国新教之间宗派仇恨的种子。19世纪中叶，爱尔兰因大饥荒出现了史上最大的移民潮，大多数移民迁往美国。因而，美国有着众多爱尔兰人的后裔，这就是为什么美国在英国和爱尔兰政治和宗教纷争中能扮演积极的调和者的角色和作用。

在文学关系上，爱尔兰戏剧的海外传播也多以美国为中心。在美国，爱尔兰拥有广大的爱尔兰后裔美国观众基础，尤其是自20世纪90年代以来，爱尔兰民族文化的海外推广更加走向自觉，很多爱尔兰剧作家，如后面章节中介绍的辛格、奥卡西、弗里尔、卡尔和麦克多纳都享有很高的国际声誉。

CHAPTER 5

威廉·巴特勒·叶芝

William Butler Yeats

《胡里痕的凯瑟琳》

Cathleen ni Houlihan

一、剧作家简介

威廉·巴特勒·叶芝（William Butler Yeats，1865—1939），爱尔兰诗人、剧作家、“爱尔兰文艺复兴运动”的领袖、阿贝剧院（Abbey Theatre）的创建者之一。叶芝出生于爱尔兰首都都柏林，父亲是前拉斐尔派（Pre-Raphaelite）的画家，从小就与各种艺术家有着频繁的接触。他的作品融合了个人对爱尔兰乡间生活和民族神话的探索和思考。

虽然中国读者很熟悉叶芝的诗歌，但对叶芝而言，他似乎更强调自己作为一个剧作家的身份。他认为戏剧是“最有效、最有力的文学形式，是对生活最生动的模仿”。作为剧作家，叶芝先后写过26部剧本。1896年，叶芝结识了贵族出身的剧作家格雷戈里夫人，开始了两人的文学合作。1899年，叶芝与格雷戈里夫人、约翰·辛格等致力于爱尔兰民族戏剧复兴的其他剧作家一起于1904年正式成立阿贝剧院。在爱尔兰文艺复兴时期，叶芝创作了一系列反映爱尔兰历史和农民生活的戏剧，代表剧作有《胡里痕的凯瑟琳》（*Cathleen ni Houlihan*，1902）、《凯瑟琳女伯爵》（*The Countess Cathleen*，1911）等。

叶芝在戏剧方面的成就体现在他促成了爱尔兰民族戏剧的发展。由他发起和创办的阿贝剧院，即当今的爱尔兰国家剧院，历经百年后成为爱尔兰文化的标志建筑，成为宝贵的精神财富。阿贝剧院在复兴和传播爱尔兰本土语言以及古爱尔兰的神话传说、历史故事方面发挥了积极的推动作用。

二、剧 情 简 介

《胡里痕的凯瑟琳》（*Cathleen ni Houlihan*）是一部独幕剧。该剧取材于爱尔兰“凯瑟琳”的古老传说故事。一日黄昏，老妇人凯瑟琳借避风雨之际，向善良的基兰一家诉说自己家园被夺的故事。她的悲惨命运打动了第二日即将成婚的青年男子迈克。迈克毅然放弃了小家，奔赴前线参战。剧尾，老妇人迈着女王般的优雅步伐，化身成了年轻的女士。

无疑，凯瑟琳这一人物形象呈现出了典型的民族象征意义，它配合了该剧故事的刻意设定——1798年“联合的爱尔兰人”起义抗英的重要历史时刻使得迈克奔赴前线的行为成为为民族解放运动献身的具象体现。

该剧是叶芝早期戏剧的代表作，更是爱尔兰民族戏剧运动中具有里程碑意义的剧作。该剧自1902 年首演成功以来，一直成为阿贝剧院的保留剧目，它是爱尔兰民族独立精神诉求的表达，更激发了爱尔兰文艺复兴时期人们的民族意识，成为爱尔兰民族戏剧舞台上爱尔兰传统象征——母亲——的经典形象。

三、名篇选读

Cathleen ni Houlihan

Characters In the Play

Peter Gillane

Michael Gillane, his son, going to be married

Patrick Gillane, a lad of twelve, Michael's brother

Bridget Gillane, Peter's wife

Delia Cahel, engaged to Michael

The poor old woman

Neighbours

(**SCENE:** *Interior of a cottage close to Kilala, in 1798. Bridget is standing at a table undoing a parcel. Peter is sitting at one side of the fire, Patrick at the other.*)

PETER: What is that sound I hear?

PATRICK: I don't hear anything. (*He listens.*) I hear it now. It's like cheering. (*He goes to the window and looks out.*) I wonder what they are cheering about. I don't see anybody.

PETER: It might be a hurling[1].

PATRICK: There's no hurling to-day. It must be down in the town the cheering is.

BRIDGET: I suppose the boys must be having some sport of their own. Come over here, Peter, and look at Michael's wedding clothes.

PETER: (*shift his chair to table*) Those are grand clothes, indeed.

BRIDGET: You hadn't clothes like that when you married me, and no coat to put on of a Sunday more than any other day.

PETER: That is true, indeed. We never thought a son of our own would be wearing a suit of that sort for his wedding, or have so good a place to bring a wife to.

PATRICK: (*who is still at the window*) There's an old women coming down the road. I don't know is it here she is coming.

BRIDGET: It will be a neighbor coming to hear about Michael's wedding. Can you see who it is?

PATRICK: I think it is a stranger, but she's not coming to the house. She's turned into the gap that goes down where Maurteen and his sons are shearing sheep. (*He turns towards Bridget.*) Do you remember what Winny of the Cross-Roads was saying the other night about the strange woman that goes through the country whatever time there's war or trouble coming?

BRIDGET: Don't be bothering us about Winny's talk, but go and open the door fir your brother. I hear him coming up the path.

PETER: I hope he has brought us about Delia's fortune with him safe, for fear the people might go back on the bargain and I after making it. Trouble enough I had making it.

(*Patrick opens the door and Michael comes in.*)

BRIDGET: What kept you, Michael? We were looking out for you all this long time.

MICHAEL: I went to the priest's house to bid him be ready to marry us to-morrow.

BRIDGET: Did he say anything?

MICHAEL: He said it was a very nice match, and he was never better pleased to marry any two in his parish than myself and Delia Cahel.

PETER: Have you got the fortune, Michael?

MICHAEL: Here it is.

(*Michael puts bag on the table and goes over and leans against chimney-jamb. Bridget, who has been all this time examining the clothes, pulling the seams and trying the lining of the pocket, etc., puts the clothes on the dresser.*)

PETER: (*getting up and taking the bag in his hand and turning out the money*) Yes, I made the bargain well for you, Michael. Old John Cahel would sooner keep a share of this while longer. 'Let me keep the half of it until the first boy is born', says he. 'You will not,' says I. 'Whatever there is or is not a boy, the whole hundred pounds must in Michael's hands before he brings your daughter to the house.' The wife spoke to him then, and he gave in at the end.

BRIDGET: You seem well pleased to be handling the money, Peter.

PETER: Indeed, I wish I had had the luck to get the hundred pounds, or twenty pounds itself, with the wife I married.

BRIDGET: Well, if I didn't bring too much I didn't get much. What had you the day I married you but a flock of hens and you feeding them, and few lambs and you driving them to the market at Ballina[2]? (*She is vexed and bangs a jug on the dresser.*) If I brought no fortune I worked it out in my bones, laying down the baby, Michael that is standing there now, on a stook of straw, while I dug the potatoes, and never asking big dresses or anything but to be working.

PETER: That is true, indeed.

(*He pats her arm.*)

BRIDGET: Leave me alone now till I ready the house for the woman that is to come into it.

PETER: You have the best woman in Ireland, but the money is good, too; (*He begins handling the money again and sits down.*) I never thought to see so much money within my four walls. We can do great things now we have it. We can take the ten acres of land we have the chance of since Jamise Dempsey died, and stock it. We will go to the fair at Ballina to buy the stock. Did Delia ask any of the money for her own use,

Michael?

MICHAEL: She did not, indeed. She did not seem to take much notice of it, or to look at it at all.

BRIDGET: That's no wonder. Why would she look at it when she had yourself to look at, a fine, strong young man? It is proud she must be to get you; a good steady boy that will make use of the money, and not be running through it or spending it on drink like another.

PETER: It's likely Michael himself was not thinking much of the fortune, either, but of what sort the girl was to look at.

MICHAEL: (*coming over towards the table*) Well, you would like a nice comely girl to be beside you, and to go walking with you. The fortune only lasts for a while, but the women will be there always.

PATRICK: (*turning round from the window*) They are cheering again down in the town. Maybe they are landing horses from Enniscrone. They do be cheering when the horses take the water well.

MICHAEL: There are no horses in it. Where would they be going and no fair at hand? Go down to the town, Patrick, and see what is going on.

PATRICK: (*opens the door to go out, but stops for a moment on the threshold*) Will Delia remember, do you think, to bring the greyhound pup she promised me when be coming to the house?

MICHAEL: She will surely.

(*Patrick goes out, leaving the door open.*)

PETER: It will be Patrick's turn next to be looking for a fortune, but he won't find it easy to get it and he with no place of his own.

BRIDGET: I do be thinking sometimes, now things are going so well with us, and the Cahels such a good back to us in the district, and Delia's own uncle a priest, we might be put in the way of making Patrick a priest some day, and he so good at his books.

PETER: Time enough, time enough. You have always your head full of plans, Bridget.

BRIDGET: We will be well able to give him learning, and not to send him tramping the country like a poor scholar that lives on charity.

MICHAEL: They're done cheering yet.

(*He goes over the door and stands there for a moment, putting up his hand to shade his eyes.*)

BRIDGET: Do you see anything?

MICHAEL: I see an old woman coming up the path.

BRIDGET: Who is it, I wonder? It must be the strange woman Patrick saw a while ago.

MICHAEL: I don't think it's one of the neighbours anyway, but she has her cloak over face.

BRIDGET: It might be some poor woman heard we were making ready for the wedding and came to look for her share.

PETER: I may as well put the money out of sight. There is no use leaving it out for every stranger to look at.

(*He goes over to a large box in the corner, opens it and puts the bag in and fumbles at the lock.*)

MICHAEL: There she is, father! (*An Old Woman passes the window slowly. She looks at Michael as she passes.*) I'd sooner a stranger not to come to the house the night before my wedding.

BRIDGET: Open the door, Michael; don't keep the poor woman waiting.

(*The Old Woman comes in; Michael stands aside to make way for her.*)

OLD WOMAN: God save all here!

PETER: God save you kindly!

OLD WOMAN: You have good shelter here.

PETER: You are welcome to whatever shelter we have.

BRIDGET: Sit down there by the fire and welcome.

OLD WOMAN: (*warming her hands*) There is a hard wind outside.

(*Michael watches her curiously from the door. Peter comes over to the table.*)

PETER: Have you travelled far to-day?

OLD WOMAN: I have travelled far; there are few have travelled so far as myself, and there's many a one that doesn't make me welcome. There was one that had strong sons I thought were friends of mine, but they were shearing their sheep, and they wouldn't listen to me.

PETER: It's a pity indeed for any person to have a place of there own.

OLD WOMAN: That's true for you indeed, and it's long I'm on the roads since I first went wandering.

BRIDGET: It's a wonder you are not worn out with so much wandering.

OLD WOMAN: Sometimes my feet are tires and my hands are quiet, but there is no quiet in my heart. They think old age has come to me and that all the stir has gone out of me. But when the trouble is on me I must be talking to my friends.

BRIDGET: What was it put you wandering?

OLD WOMAN: Too many strangers in the house.

BRIDGET: Indeed you look as if you'd had your share of trouble.

OLD WOMAN: I have had trouble indeed.

BRIDGET: What was it put the trouble on you?

OLD WOMAN: My land that was broken from me.

PETER: Was it much land they took from you?

OLD WOMAN: My four beautiful green fields.

PETER: (*aside to Bridget*) Do you think could she be the widow Casey that was put out of her holding at Kilglass a while ago?

BRIDGET: She is not. I saw the widow Casey one time at the market in Ballina, a stout fresh woman.

PETER: (*to Old Women*) Did you hear a noise of cheering, and you coming up the hill?

OLD WOMAN: I thought I heard the noise I used to hear when my friends came to visit me.

(*She begins singing half to herself.*)

I will go cry with the woman,
Four yellow-haired Donough is dead,
With a hempen rope for a neckcloth.

And a white cloth on his head —

MICHAEL: (*coming from the door*) What is it that you are singing, ma'am?

OLD WOMAN: Singing I am about a man I knew one time, yellow-haired Donough that was hanged in Galway[3].

(*She goes on singing, much louder.*)

I am come to cry with you, woman,
My hair is unwound and unbound;
I remember him ploughing his field,
Turning up the red side of the ground,
And building his barn on the hill,
With the good mortared stone,
O! we'd have pulled down the gallows;
Had it happened in Enniscrone!

MICHAEL: What was it brought him to his death?

OLD WOMAN: He died for love of me; many a man has died for love of me.

PETER: (*aside to Bridget*) Her trouble has put her wits astray.

MICHAEL: Is it long since that song was made? Is it long since he got his death?

OLD WOMAN: Not long, not long. But there were others that died for love of me a long time ago.

MICHAEL: Were they neighbours of your own, ma'am?

OLD WOMAN: Come here beside me and I'll tell you about them. (*Michael sits down beside her on the hearth.*) There was a red man of the O'Donnells from the north, and a man of the O'Sullivans from the south, and there was one Brian that lost his life at Clontarf[4] by the sea, and there were a great many on the west, some that died hundreds of years ago, and there are some that died hundreds of years ago, and there are some that will die to-morrow.[5]

MICHAEL: Is it in the west that men will die to-morrow?

OLD WOMAN: Come nearer, nearer to me.

BRIDGET: Is she right, do you think? Or is she a woman from beyond the world?

PETER: She doesn't know well that she'd talking about, with the want and the trouble she has gone through.

BRIDGET: The poor thing, we should treat her well.

PETER: Give her a drink if milk and a bit of the oaten cake.

BRIDGET: Maybe we should give her something along with that, to bring her on her way. A few pence or a shilling itself, and we with so much money in the house.

PETER: Indeed I'd not begrudge it to her if we had it to spare, but if we go running through what we have, we'll soon have to break the hundred pounds, and that would be a pity.

BRIDGET: Shame on you, Peter. Give her the shilling and your blessing with it, or our own luck will go from us.

(*Peter goes to the box and takes out a shilling.*)

BRIDGET: (*to the Old Woman*) Will you have a drink of milk, ma'am?

OLD WOMAN: It is not food or drink that I want.

PETER: (*offering the shilling*) Here is some for you.

OLD WOMAN: That is not what I want. It is not silver I want.

PETER: What is it you would be asking for?

OLD WOMAN: If anyone would give me help he must give me himself, he must give me all.

(*Peter goes over to the table staring at the shilling in his hand in a bewildered way, and stands whispering to Bridget.*)

MICHAEL: Have you no one to care you in your age, ma'am?

OLD WOMAN: I have not. With all the lovers that brought me their love I never set out the bed for any.

MICHAEL: Are you lonely going the roads, ma'am?

OLD WOMAN: The hope of getting my beautiful fields back again; the hope of putting the strangers out of my house.

MICHAEL: What way will you do that, ma'am?

OLD WOMAN: I have good friends that will help me. They are gathering to help me now. I am not afraid. If they are put down to-day they will get the upper hand to-morrow. (*She gets up.*) I must be going to meet my friends. They are coming to help me and I must be there to welcome them. I must call the neighbours together to welcome them.

MICHAEL: I will go with you.

BRIDGET: It is not her friends you have to go and welcome, Michael; it is the girl coming into the house you have to welcome. You have plenty to do; it is food and drink you have to bring to the house. The woman that is coming home is not coming with empty hands; you would not have an empty house before her. (*to the Old Woman*) Maybe you don't know, ma'am, that my son is going to be married to-morrow.

OLD WOMAN: It is not a man going to his marriage that I look to for help.

PETER: (*to Bridget*) You did not tell your name yet, ma'am.

OLD WOMAN: Some call me the Poor Old Woman, and there are some that call me Cathleen, the daughter of Houlihan[6].

PETER: I think I know someone of that name, once. Who was it, I wonder? It must have been someone I knew when I was a boy. No, no; I remember, I heard it in a song.

OLD WOMAN: (*who is standing in the doorway*) They are wondering that there were songs made for me; there have been many songs made for me. I heard one on the wind this morning.

(*sings*)

Do not make a great keening
When the graves have been dug to-morrow.
Do not call the white-scarfed riders
To the burying that shall be to-morrow.

Do not spread food to call strangers
To the wakes that shall be to-morrow.
Do not give money for prayers
For the dead that shall die to-morrow.
They will have no need of prayers, they will have no need of prayers.

MICHAEL: I do not know what that song means, but tell me something I can do for you.

PETER: Come over to me, Michael.

MICHAEL: Hush, father, listen to her.

OLD WOMAN: It is a hard service they take that help me. Many that are red-cheeked now will be pale-cheeked; many that have been free to walk the hills and the bogs and the rushes will be sent to walk hard streets in far countries; many a good plan will be broken; many that have gathered, money will not stay to spend it; many a child will be born and there will be no father at its christening to give it a name. They that have red cheeks will have pale cheeks for my sake, and for all that, they will think they are well paid.[7]

(*She goes out; her voice is heard outside singing.*)

They shall be remembered for ever;
They shall be alive for ever;
They shall be speaking foe ever;
The people shall hear them for ever.

BRIDGET: (*to Peter*) Look at him, Peter; he had the look of a man that has got the touch. (*Raising her voice.*) Look here, Michael, at the wedding clothes. Such grand clothes as these are! You have a right to fit them on now; it would be a pity to-morrow if they did not fit. The boys would be laughing at you. Take them, Michael, and go into the room and fit them on.

(*She puts them on his arm.*)

MICHAEL: What wedding are you talking of? What clothes will I be wearing to-morrow?

BRIDGET: These are the clothes you are going to wear when you marry Delia Cahel to-morrow.

MICHAEL: I had forgotten that.

(*He looks at the clothes and turns towards the inner room, but stops at the sound of cheering outside.*)

PETER: There is the shouting come to our own door. What is it has happened?

(*Neighbours come crowding in, Patrick and Delia with them.*)

PATRICK: There are ships in the Bay; the French are landing at Killala[8]!

(*Peter takes his pipe from his mouth and his hat off, and stands up. The clothes slip from Michael's arm.*)

DELIA: Michael! (*He takes no notice.*) Michael! (*He turn towards.*) Why do you look at me like a stranger?

(*She drops his arm. Bridget goes over towards her.*)

PATRICK: The boys are all hurrying down the hillside to join the French.

DELIA: Michael won't be going to join the French.

BRIDGET: (*to Peter*) Tell him not to go, Peter.

PETER: It's no use. He doesn't hear a word we're saying.

BRIDGET: Try and coax him over to the fire.

DELIA: Michael, Michael! You won't leave me! You won' t leave me! You won't join the French, and we are going to be married!

(*She puts her arms about him, he turns towards her as if about to yield.*)

(*Old Woman's voice outside.*)

They shall be speaking for ever;
The people shall hear for ever.

(*Michael breaks away from Delia, stands for a second at the door, then rushes out, following the Old Woman's voice. Bridget takes Delia, who is crying silently, into her arms.*)

PETER: (*to Patrick, laying a hand on his arm*) Did you see an old woman going down the path?

PATRICK: I did not, but I see a young girl, and she had the walk of a queen.

注释

1. **hurling:** 爱尔兰曲棍球。该项运动在爱尔兰广受欢迎，是一项历史悠久的运动。
2. **Ballina:** 巴里纳，爱尔兰共和国西北部梅欧郡（Mayo）的最大城镇。
3. **Galway:** 戈尔韦，爱尔兰西部的港口城市。

4. **Clontarf:** 克朗塔夫，爱尔兰城市，位于都柏林附近。本处暗指1014年的克朗塔夫战役（Battle of Clontarf）。

5. 本段话里老妇人将爱尔兰历史上著名的反抗运动和当下的抗争相结合，表明了爱尔兰人民从古至今、不屈不挠的反抗精神，显得意味深长。

6. **Houlihan:** 胡里痕，爱尔兰传统姓氏，盖尔语姓氏的英语形式，意思是“骄傲的”（proud, arrogant）。该姓氏赋予老妇人很强的象征寓意。

7. 本处老妇人寓指很多爱尔兰人在抗争中前赴后继，并为此而牺牲。

8. **Killala:** 基拉拉，爱尔兰梅欧郡（Mayo）的一个小镇，位于前文所提及的巴里纳的北部。

四、拓展思考

1. Near the end, Patrick said that “I did not, but I see a young girl, and she had the walk of a queen.” How do you understand Patrick’s description of Cathleen, the old woman?

2. How do you interpret the characterization of “the Old Woman”? What kind of symbolic significance does the characterization stand for?

3. Please state the reason why the playwright sets the story in the year of 1798.

五、延展阅读

《胡里痕的凯瑟琳》是叶芝根据古盖尔传说改编而成的独幕剧，也有说法认为该剧是叶芝和阿贝剧院的另一位重要创建者格雷戈里夫人共同合作而成的。更为重要的是，1902年该剧在都柏林首演时，担任女主角的是年轻漂亮的女演员毛特·岗（Maut Gunn）——叶芝一生倾慕并为之写下《当你老了》（*When you are old*）名诗的女人。

叶芝一直致力于发扬爱尔兰古老传统，并从历史、传统中寻找文化养分，创建爱尔兰民族剧院，意欲彻底改变英国戏剧舞台上被歪曲和异化的爱尔兰人和爱尔兰民族形象——好斗、懒惰，并呈现了真正的爱尔兰人形象——勤劳、善良，直面苦难。自此，以阿贝剧院舞台为核心阵地，爱尔兰戏剧走上民族化发展道路，涌现了如辛格、奥卡西为首的戏剧大家。

读者可以将第1章《亨利五世》中的爱尔兰军官麦克·莫里斯的形象与叶芝戏剧中的形象进行比较。细心的读者还可以从英国经典作家们的笔下寻找爱尔兰的形象，如夏洛蒂·勃朗特的《简·爱》，读者从中可以看到英格兰作家中心主义的“无意识”显现。

一种文学现象总是需要与之相隔一段距离，才可以更为“冷峻”地审视。在21世纪回望和反思100年前叶芝所倡导的爱尔兰戏剧运动，一方面可以看到当时爱尔兰戏剧民族化之于爱尔兰民族解放、民族文化发展的时代意义和文化价值；但另一方面，一味地在爱尔兰舞台上塑造豪迈的爱尔兰英雄和温馨的爱尔兰绿色田园，造成文学艺术形象单一，很大程度又体现了这一时期戏剧运动的时代局限性。也正是这一局限性，使得萧伯纳一度被排除在爱尔兰作家行列，与辛格、奥卡西一样，在20世纪上半叶一度不为爱尔兰观众接受和认同（详见第6章辛格和第8章奥卡西）。

CHAPTER 6

约翰·米林顿·辛格

John Millington Synge

《骑马下海的人》

Riders to the Sea

一、剧作家简介

约翰·米林顿·辛格（John Millington Synge，1871—1909）是20世纪爱尔兰文艺复兴时期著名的剧作家。1871年辛格出生于都柏林郊外威克洛（Wicklow）的一个新教地主家庭。他自幼喜爱音乐，并因这一爱好前往德国进修。此外，他深谙爱尔兰语，是20世纪初爱尔兰文艺复兴时期不可多得的爱尔兰古语言和文化专家。因与叶芝结识并深受叶芝振兴爱尔兰民族戏剧思想的影响，辛格积极投身阿贝剧院的创建工作，为阿贝奉献他的戏剧作品。

辛格的重要剧作有：《西方世界的花花公子》（*The Playboy of the Western World*，1907）、《骑马下海的人》（*Riders to the Sea*，1904）、《峡谷的阴影》（*In the Shadow of the Glen*，1903）、《补锅匠的婚礼》（*The Tinker's Wedding*，1908）、《圣泉》（*The Well of the Saints*，1905）等优秀作品。辛格着眼于爱尔兰西部贫困的现实生活（尤其是以阿兰岛为中心）和普通人困境重压之下的精神世界，他的戏剧具有强烈的现实感和象征意义。

辛格认为生活是戏剧的唯一源泉，他把真实地反映爱尔兰农民的生活作为他戏剧创作的主要任务。但也由于辛格笔下的爱尔兰农民形象呈现出的滑稽、荒唐、可笑的一面，如最为著名的“花花公子”形象，在当时努力树立爱尔兰人“真实的正面形象”的文化语境下，招致众人的抨击。但历史证明，辛格独特且富于乐感的爱尔兰式英语和诙谐而夸张的人物造型之于其严肃的民族特性发掘出的戏剧探索之路是成功的。辛格与叶芝、奥卡西一起成为20世纪上半叶爱尔兰戏剧的杰出代表。

二、剧情简介

《骑马下海的人》是辛格的代表剧作之一，是一部独幕剧。戏剧场景设在爱尔兰西部的一个小岛。岛上的人们跨海去对岸的集市进行交易，靠着微薄的收入维持生活。但海上的风浪成为吞噬人们生命的杀手。该剧以简洁的笔墨和虚实相间的结构技巧，着重描写了毛里亚的两个儿子迈克（Michael）和巴特利（Bartley）之死，由此引出毛里亚经历丈夫、公公和6个儿子先后葬身大海的痛苦回忆，揭示了爱尔兰渔民世代相继的悲惨命运。

该剧通过将现实与历史回顾相结合的情节设计，既有效地将现实悲情延展至周而复始的悲剧轮回，营造出浓重的悲剧意境，又实现了独幕剧高度凝练和集中的形式要求，因此，该剧被誉为20世纪最优秀的独幕悲剧。此外，在塑造母亲形象方面，老妇人的形象继承了叶芝在《胡里痕的凯瑟琳》中的老妇人（母亲）这一民族形象的传统象征意义，并呈现出刚毅的精神品质，这在20世纪上半叶爱尔兰文艺复兴运动的戏剧舞台上是具有历史意义的。

三、名篇选读

Riders to the Sea

Characters in the Play

Maurya, an old woman

Bartley, her son

Cathleen, her daughter

Nora, a younger daughter

Men and women

Scene

An Island off the West of Ireland

First Production

(Dublin, 25 February, 1904)

Maurya Honor Lavelle

Bartley W. G. Fay

Cathleen Sara Allgood

Nora Emma Vernon

Men and women P. J. Kelly, Seamus O'Sullivan, George Roberts, Maire Nic Shiubhlaigh, and Doreen Gunning

(Cottage kitchen, with nets, oil-skins, spinning wheel, some new boards standing by the wall, etc. Cathleen, a girl of about twenty, finishes kneading cake, and puts it down in the pot-oven by the fire, then wipes her hands, and begins to spin at the wheel. Nora, a young girl, puts her head in at the door.)

NORA: (*in a low voice*) Where is she[1]?

CATHLEEN: She's lying down. God help her, and maybe sleeping, if she's able.[2]

(Nora comes in softly, and takes a bundle from under her shawl.)

CATHLEEN: (*spinning the wheel rapidly*) What is it you have?

NORA: The young priest is after bringing them. It's a shirt and a plain stocking were got off a drowned man in Donegal[3].

(Cathleen stops her wheel with a sudden movement, and leans out to listen.)

NORA: We're to find out if it's Michael's some time herself will be down looking by the sea.

CATHLEEN: How would they be Michael's, Nora. How would he go the length of that way to the far north?

NORA: The young priest says he's known the like of it. "If it's Michael's," says he, "you can tell herself he's got a clean burial by the grace of God, and if they're not his, let no one say a word about them, for she'll be getting her death," says he, "with crying and lamenting."

(The door which Nora half closed behind her is blown open by a gust of wind.)

CATHLEEN: (*looking out anxiously*) Did you ask him would he stop Bartley going this day with the horses to the Galway fair?

NORA: "I won't stop him," says he, "but let you not be afraid. Herself does be saying prayers half through the night, and the Almighty God won't leave her destitute[4]," says he, "with no son living."

CATHLEEN: Is the sea bad by the white rocks, Nora?

NORA: Middling bad, God help us. There's a great roaring in the west, and it's worse it'll be getting when the tide's turned to the wind.

(*She goes over to the table with the bundle.*) **Shall I open it now?**

CATHLEEN: Maybe she'd wake up on us, and come in before we'd done. (*coming to the table*) It's a long time we'll be, and the two of us crying.

NORA: (*goes to the inner door and listens*) She's moving about on the bed. She'll be coming in a minute.

CATHLEEN: Give me the ladder, and I'll put them up in the turf-loft. The way she won't know of them at all, and maybe when the tide turns she'll be going down to see would he be floating from the east.

(*They put the ladder against the gable of the chimney. Cathleen goes up a few steps and hides the bundle in the turf-loft. Maurya comes from the inner room.*)

MAURYA: (*looking up at Cathleen and speaking querulously*) Isn't it turf enough you have for this day and evening?

CATHLEEN: There's a cake baking at the fire for a short space (*throwing down the turf*), and Bartley will want it when the tide turns if he goes to Connemara[5].

(*Nora picks up the turf and puts it round the pot-oven.*)

MAURYA: (*sitting down on a stool at the fire*) He[6] won't go this day with the wind rising from the south and west. He won't go this day, for the young priest will stop him surely.

NORA: He'll not stop him, mother, and I heard Eamon Simon and Stephen Pheety and Colum Shawn saying he would go[7].

MAURYA: Where is he itself?

NORA: He went down to see would there be another boat sailing in the week, and I'm thinking it won't be long till he's here now, for the tide's turning at the green head, and the hooker's tacking from the east.

CATHLEEN: I hear someone passing the big stones.

NORA: (*looking out*) He's coming now, and he in a hurry.

BARTLEY: (*comes in and looks round the room, speaking sadly and quietly*) Where is the bit of new rope, Cathleen, was bought in Connemara?

CATHLEEN: (*coming down*) Give it to him, Nora; it's on a nail by the white boards. I hung it up this morning, for the pig with the black feet was eating it.

NORA: (*giving him a rope*) Is that it, Bartley?

MAURYA: (*as before*) You'd do right to leave that rope, Bartley, hanging by the boards. (*Bartley takes the rope.*) It will be wanting in this place, I'm telling you. If Michael is washed up tomorrow morning, or the next morning, or any morning in the week, for it's a deep grave we'll make him by the grace of God.

BARTLEY: (*beginning to work with the rope*) I've no halter the way I can ride down on the mare, and I must go now quickly. This is the one boat going for two weeks or beyond it, and the fair will be a good fair for horses I heard them saying below.

MAURYA: It's a hard thing they'll be saying below if the body is washed up and there's no man in it to make the coffin, and I after giving a big price for the finest white boards you'd find in Connemara. (*She looks round at the boards.*)

BARTLEY: How would it be washed up, and we after looking each day for nine days, and a strong wind blowing a while back from the west and south?

MAURYA: If it isn't found itself, that wind is raising the sea, and there was a star up against the moon, and it rising in the night. If it was a hundred horses, or a thousand horses you had itself, what is the price of a thousand horses against a son where there is one son only?

BARTLEY: (*walking at the halter, to Cathleen*) Let you go down each day, and see the sheep aren't jumping in on the rye, and if the jobber comes you can sell the pig with the black feet if there is a good price going.

MAURYA: How would the like of her get a good price for a pig?

BARTLEY: (*to Cathleen*) If the west wind holds with the last bit of the moon, let you and Nora get up weed enough for another cock for the kelp. It's hard set we'll be from this day with no one in but one man to work.

MAURYA: It's hard set we'll be surely the day you're drown'd with the rest. What way will I live and the girls with me, and I an old woman looking for the grave?

(*Bartley lays down the halter, takes off his old coat, and puts on a newer one of the same flannel.*)

BARTLEY: (*to Nora*) Is she coming to the pier?

NORA: (*looking out*) She's passing the green head and letting fall her sails.

BARTLEY: (*getting his purse and tobacco*) I'll have half an hour to go down, and you'll see me coming again in two days, or in three days, or maybe in four days if the wind is bad.

MAURYA: (*turning round to the fire, and putting her shawl over her head*) Isn't it a hard cruel man won't hear a word from an old woman, and she holding him from the sea?

CATHLEEN: It's the life of a young man to be going on the sea, and who would listen to an old woman with one thing and she saying it over?

BARTLEY: (*taking the halter*) I must go now quickly. I'll ride down on the red mare, and the grey pony'll run behind me... The blessing of God on you. (*He goes out.*)

MAURYA: (*crying out as he is in the door way*) He's gone now. God spare us, and we'll not see him again. He's gone now, and when the black bight is falling I'll have no son left me in the world.[8]

CATHLEEN: Why wouldn't you give him your blessing and he looking round in the door? Isn't it sorrow enough is on every one in the house without your sending him out with an unlucky word behind him, and a hard word in his ear?

(*Maurya takes up the tongs and begins raking the fire aimlessly without looking round.*)

NORA: (*turning towards her*) You're taking away the turf from the cake.

CATHLEEN: (*crying out*) The Son of God forgive us, Nora. we're after forgetting his bit of bread. (*She comes over to the fire.*)

NORA: And it's destroyed he'll be going till dark night, and he after eating nothing since the sun went up.

CATHLEEN: (*turning the cake out of the oven*) It's destroyed he'll be, surely. There's no sense left on any person in a house where an old woman will be talking forever.

(*Maurya sways herself on her stool.*)

CATHLEEN: (*cutting off some of the bread and rolling it in a cloth, to Maurya*) Let you go down now to the spring well and give him this and he passing. You'll see him then and the dark word will be broken, and you can say "God speed you", the way he'll be easy in his mind.

MAURYA: (*taking the bread*) Will I be in it as soon as himself?

CATHLEEN: If you go now quickly.

MAURYA: (*standing up unsteadily*) It's hard set I am to walk.

CATHLEEN: (*looking at her anxiously*) Give her the stick, Nora, or maybe she'll slip on the big stones.

NORA: What stick?

CATHLEEN: The stick Michael brought from Connemara.

MAURYA: (*taking a stick Nora gives her*) In the big world the old people do be leaving things after them for their sons and children, but in this place it is the young men do be leaving things behind for them that do be old. (*She goes out slowly.*)

(*Nora goes over to the ladder.*)

CATHLEEN: Wait, Nora. Maybe she'd turn back quickly. She's that sorry, God help her, you wouldn't know the thing she'd do.

NORA: Is she gone round by the bush?

CATHLEEN: (*looking out*) She's gone now. Throw it down quickly, for the Lord knows when she'll be out of it again.

NORA: (*getting the bundle from the loft*) The young priest said he'd be passing tomorrow, and we might go down and speak to him below if it's Michael's they are surely.

CATHLEEN: (*taking the bundle from Nora*) Did he say what way they were found?

NORA: (*coming down*) "There were two men," says he, "and they rowing round with poteen before the cocks crowed, and the oar of one of them caught the body, and they passing the black cliffs of the north."

CATHLEEN: (*trying to open the bundle*) Give me a knife, Nora. The string's perished with the salt water, and there's a black knot on it you wouldn't loosen in a week.

NORA: (*giving her a knife*) I've heard that it was a long way to Donegal.

CATHLEEN: (*cutting the string*) It is surely. There was a man in here a while ago—the man sold us that knife—and he said if you set off walking from the rocks beyond, it would be in seven days you'd be in Donegal.

NORA: And what time would a man take, and he floating?

(*Cathleen opens the bundle and takes out a bit of a shirt and a stocking. They look at them eagerly.*)

CATHLEEN: (*in a low voice*) The Lord spare us, Nora! Isn't it a queer hard thing to say if it's his they are surely?

NORA: I'll get his shirt off the hook the way we can put the one flannel on the other. (*She looks through some clothes hanging in the corner.*) It's not with them, Cathleen, and where will it be?

CATHLEEN: I'm thinking Bartley put it on him in the morning, for his own shirt was heavy with the salt in it. (*pointing to the corner*) There's a bit of a sleeve was of the same stuff. Give me that and it will do.

(*Nora brings it to her and they compare the flannel.*)

CATHLEEN: It's the same stuff, Nora; but if it is itself aren't there great rolls of it in the shops of Galway, and isn't it many another man may have a shirt of it as well as Michael himself?

NORA: (*who has taken up the stocking and counted the stitches, crying out*) It's Michael, Cathleen, it's Michael. God spare his soul, and what will herself say when she hears this story, and Bartley on the sea?

CATHLEEN: (*taking the stocking*) It's a plain stocking.

NORA: It's the second one of the third pair I knitted, and I put up three score stitches, and I dropped four of them.

CATHLEEN: (*counts the stitches*) It's that number is in it. (*crying out*) Ah, Nora, isn't it a bitter thing to think of him floating that way to the far north, and no one to keen him but the black hags that do be flying on the sea?

NORA: (*swinging herself round and throwing out her arms on the clothes*) And isn't it a pitiful thing when there is nothing left of a man who was a great rower and fisher, but a bit of an old shirt and a plain stocking?

CATHLEEN: (*after an instant*) Tell me is herself coming, Nora? I hear a little sound on the path.

NORA: (*looking out*) She is, Cathleen. She's coming up to the door.

CATHLEEN: Put these things away before she'll come in. Maybe it's easier she'll be after giving her blessing to Bartley, and we won't let on we've heard anything the time he's on the sea.

NORA: (*helping Cathleen to close the bundle*) We'll put them here in the corner. (*They put them into a hole in the chimney corner. Cathleen goes back to the spinning-wheel.*)

NORA: Will she see it was crying I was?

CATHLEEN: Keep your back to the door the way the light'll not be on you.

(*Nora sits down at the chimney corner, with her back to the door. Maurya comes in very slowly, without looking at the girls, and goes over to her stool at the other side of the fire. The cloth with the bread is still in her hand. The girls look at each other, and Nora points to the bundle of bread.*)

CATHLEEN: (*after spinning for a moment*) You didn't give him his bit of bread?

(*Maurya begins to keen softly, without turning round.*)

CATHLEEN: Did you see him riding down?

(*Maurya goes on keening.*)

CATHLEEN: (*a little impatiently*) God forgive you; isn't it a better thing to raise your voice and tell what you seen, than to be making lamentation for a thing that's done? Did you see Bartley, I'm saying to you.

MAURYA: (*with a weak voice*) My heart's broken from this day.

CATHLEEN: (*as before*) Did you see Bartley?

MAURYA: I seen the fearfulest thing.[9]

CATHLEEN: (*leaves her wheel and looks out*) God forgive you; he's riding the mare now over the green head, and the grey pony behind him.

MAURYA: (*starts, so that her shawl falls back from her head and shows her white tossed hair, with a frightened voice*) The grey pony behind him...

CATHLEEN: (*coming to the fire*) What is it ails you, at all?

MAURYA: (*speaking very slowly*) I've seen the fearfulest thing any person has seen, since the day Bride Dara seen the dead man with the child in his arms.

CATHLEEN and NORA: Uah. (*They crouch down in front of the old woman at the fire.*)

NORA: Tell us what it is you seen.

MAURYA: I went down to the spring well, and I stood there saying a prayer to myself. Then Bartley came along, and he riding on the red mare with the gray pony behind him. (*She puts up her hands, as if to hide something from her eyes.*) The Son of God spare us, Nora!

CATHLEEN: What is it you seen.

MAURYA: I seen Michael himself.

CATHLEEN: (*speaking softly*) You did not, mother; it wasn't Michael you seen, for his body is after being found in the far north, and he's got a clean burial by the grace of God.

MAURYA: (*a little defiantly*) I'm after seeing him this day, and he riding and galloping. Bartley came first on the red mare; and I tried to say "God speed you," but something choked the words in my throat. He went by quickly; and "the blessing of God on you," says he, and I could say nothing. I looked up then, and I crying, at the gray pony, and there was Michael upon it—with fine clothes on him, and new shoes on his feet.

CATHLEEN: (*begins to keen*) It's destroyed we are from this day. It's destroyed, surely.

NORA: Didn't the young priest say the Almighty God wouldn't leave her destitute with no son living?

MAURYA: (*in a low voice, but clearly*) It's little the like of him knows of the sea... Bartley will be lost now, and let you call in Eamon and make me a good coffin out of the white boards, for I won't live after them. I've had a husband, and a husband's father, and six sons in this house—six fine men, though it was a hard birth I had with every one of them and they coming to the world—and some of them were found and some of them were not found, but they're gone now the lot of them... There were Stephen, and Shawn, were lost in the great wind, and found after in the Bay of Gregory of the Golden Mouth, and carried up the two of them on one plank, and in by that door.

(*She pauses for a moment; the girls start as if they heard something through the door that is half open behind them.*)

NORA: (*in a whisper*) Did you hear that, Cathleen? Did you hear a noise in the north-east?

CATHLEEN: (*in a whisper*) There's someone after crying out by the seashore.

MAURYA: (*continues without hearing anything*) There was Sheamus and his father, and his own father again, were lost in a dark night, and not a stick or sign was seen of them when the sun went up. There was Patch after was drowned out of a curagh that turned over. I was sitting here with Bartley, and he a baby, lying on my two knees, and I seen two women, and three women, and four women coming in, and they crossing themselves, and not saying a word. I looked out then, and there were men coming after them, and they holding a thing in the half of a red sail, and water dripping out of it—it was a dry day, Nora—and leaving a track to the door.[10]

(*She pauses again with her hand stretched out towards the door. It opens softly and old women begin to come in, crossing themselves on the threshold, and kneeling down in front of the stage with red petticoats over their heads.*)

MAURYA: (*half in a dream, to Cathleen*) Is it Patch, or Michael, or what is it at all?

CATHLEEN: Michael is after being found in the far north, and when he is found there how could he be here in this place?

MAURYA: There does be a power of young men floating round in the sea, and what way would they know if it was Michael they had, or another man like him. For when a man is nine days in the sea, and the wind blowing, it's hard set his own mother would be to say what man was in it.

CATHLEEN: It's Michael, God spare him. For they're after sending us a bit of his clothes from the far north.[11]

(*She reaches out and hands Maurya the clothes that belonged to Michael. Maurya stands up slowly, and takes them into her hands. Nora looks out.*)

NORA: They're carrying a thing among them and there's water dripping out of it and leaving a track by the big stones.

CATHLEEN: (*in a whisper to the women who have come in.*) Is it Bartley it is?

ONE OF THE WOMEN: It is surely. God rest his soul.[12]

(*Two younger women come in and pull out the table. Then men carry in the body of Bartley, laid on a plank, with a bit of a sail over it, and lay it on the table.*)

CATHLEEN: (*to the women, as they are doing so*) What way was he drowned?

ONE OF THE WOMEN: The grey pony knocked him into the sea, and he was washed out where there is a great surf on the white rocks.

(*Maurya has gone over and knelt down at the head of the table. The women are keening softly and swaying themselves with a slow movement. Cathleen and Nora kneel at the other end of the table. The men kneel near the door.*)

MAURYA: (*raising her head and speaking as if she did not see the people around her*) They're all gone now, and there isn't anything more the sea can do to me... I'll have no call now to be up crying and praying when the wind breaks from the south, and you can hear the surf is in the east, and the surf is in the west, making a great stir with the two noises, and they hitting one on the other. I'll have no call now to be going down and getting Holy Water in the dark nights after Samhain, and I won't care what way the sea is when the other women will be keening. (*to Nora*) Give me the Holy Water, Nora.

There's a small sup still on the dresser. (*Nora gives it to her.*) *Maurya drops Michael's clothes across Bartley's feet, and sprinkles the Holy Water over him.*) It isn't that I haven't prayed for you, Bartley, to the Almighty God. It isn't that I haven't said prayers in the dark night till you wouldn't know what I'd be saying; but it's a great rest I'll have now, and it's time surely. It's a great rest I'll have now, and great sleeping in the long nights after Samhain, if it's only a bit of wet flour we do have to eat, and maybe a fish that would be stinking. (*She kneels down again, crossing herself, and saying prayers under her breath.*)[13]

CATHLEEN: (*to an old man kneeling near her*) Maybe yourself and Eamon would make a coffin when the sun rises. We have fine white boards herself bought. God help her, thinking Michael would be found, and I have a new cake you can eat while you'll be working.

THE OLD MAN: (*looking at the boards*) Are there nails with them?

CATHLEEN: There are not, Colum; we didn't think of the nails.

ANOTHER MAN: It's a great wonder she wouldn't think of the nails, and all the coffins she's seen made already.

CATHLEEN: It's getting old she is, and broken.

(*Maurya stands up again very slowly and spreads out the pieces of Michael's clothes beside the body, sprinkling them with the last of the Holy Water.*)

NORA: (*in a whisper to Cathleen*) She's quiet now and easy; but the day Michael was drowned you could hear her crying out from this to the spring well. It's fonder she was of Michael, and would any one have thought that?

CATHLEEN: (*slowly and clearly*) An old woman will soon be tired with anything she will do, and isn't it nine days herself is after crying, and keening, and making great sorrow in the house?

MAURYA: (*puts the empty cup mouth downwards on the table, and lays her hands together on Bartley's feet*) They're all together this time, and the end is come. May the Almighty God have mercy on Bartley's soul, and on Michael's soul, and on the souls of Sheamus and Patch, and

Stephen and Shawn (*bending her head*) and may He have mercy on my soul, Nora, and on the soul of everyone is left living in the world. (*She pauses, and the keen rises a little more loudly from the women, then sinks away, continuing.*) Michael has a clean burial in the far north, by the grace of the Almighty God. Bartley will have a fine coffin out of the white boards, and a deep grave surely. What more can we want than that? No man at all can be living for ever, and we must be satisfied.

(*She kneels down again and the curtain falls slowly.*)

注释

1. **she:** 指诺娜和凯瑟琳的母亲毛里亚。
2. 此处凯瑟琳是指母亲毛里亚刚得知儿子迈克可能命丧大海的消息，独自在房间里悲伤，难以入睡。
3. **Donegal:** 多尼戈尔郡，位于爱尔兰西北部。
4. **destitute:** 穷困。
5. **Connemara:** 康内马拉，爱尔兰沿海地区，周围有众多小型半岛和城镇，海岸线曲折，风光险峻。
6. **He:** 指巴特利。
7. 此处指诺娜提及巴特利不顾糟糕的天气，执意出海赶集的事。
8. 此处指毛里亚预感到巴特利此行也将命丧大海。
9. 此处指毛里亚即将告诉两个女儿，她看见迈克的魂灵骑在巴特利身后的小马上这一可怕的事情。
10. 此处指毛里亚提及这个家庭的悲惨遭遇，即她的公公、丈夫和几个儿子先后命丧大海的事。
11. 此处指村民带来了迈克死去的确切消息。
12. 此处指村民同时也带来了巴特利的尸体。
13. 此处指悲伤过度的毛里亚却出奇得平静下来。“They're all gone now, and there isn't anything more the sea can do to me.”这句话意味深长。

四、拓展思考

1. What is the theme of this play?
2. Try to compare the image of Mother both in this play and in Yeats' *Cathleen ni Houlihan*. Please state the similarities and dissimilarities.
3. Please notice the features in language which are typically representations of Irish-English. Try to point out the main features and significance in this kind of hybrid.

五、延展阅读

辛格的戏剧创作多以爱尔兰西部岛屿阿兰群岛（The Aran Island）为场景，运用西部方言展现那里的人民（主要是农民和渔民）的生活。辛格笔下的人物是丰富而且多层次的，比如能说会道、具有诗人气质的农民，自由散漫、小偷小摸的补锅匠，饱受粗鲁、孤独和困倦的农民。辛格对他们虽然深表同情，但并不感伤；着眼于再现他们的苦难和悲剧，但又不失人物面对残酷现实的倔强和憧憬。无疑，辛格笔下的人物塑造既有着与20世纪初爱尔兰的戏剧运动一致的理念，又有基于现实主义丰富性的突破，从而展现了辛格心中的农民形象——世纪苦难压迫下的自卑、迷信和粗暴，骨子里不灭的热情、粗犷和不妥协。这一双面性的爱尔兰人形象在辛格的代表作《西方世界的花花公子》中体现得最为明显。

CHAPTER 7

萨缪尔·贝克特

Samuel Beckett

《来来往往》

Come and Go

一、剧作家简介

萨缪尔·贝克特（Samuel Beckett，1906—1989）出生于爱尔兰首都都柏林的一个犹太家庭，父亲是测量员，母亲是虔诚的教徒。青少年时期，他去巴黎旅游时结识了詹姆斯·乔伊斯（James Joyce，1882—1941），担任了乔伊斯的秘书，并立志做一个乔伊斯式的小说家。因此他在小说创作上深受乔伊斯的影响，有“小乔伊斯”之称。贝克特的创作类型包括戏剧、小说和诗歌，其中尤以戏剧成就最高。1969年，他因“以奇特形式的小说和戏剧作品，使现代人从精神困乏中得到振奋”而获得诺贝尔文学奖。

贝克特一生的创作经历，以1952年话剧《等待戈多》（*En attendant Godot*）的上演为标志被划分为前后两个时期。前期贝克特主要创作小说，后期则主要是写剧本。作为荒诞派戏剧的创始人之一和集大成者，贝克特一生共创作了30多个舞台剧本，其中有20多个被拍成电视剧或电影，其中最重要的三部作品是《等待戈多》（*En attendant Godot*，1952）、《剧终》（*Endgame*，1956）和《啊，美好的日子！》（*Happy Days*，1961）。他的文学作品力图通过某种追寻和这种追寻的一无所获来说明世界的荒诞和无意义。

贝克特一生的最高成就体现在他对荒诞派戏剧做出的贡献。正是因为他的一系列优秀剧作，使得荒诞派戏剧可以成为一个独立的、壮大的文学流派跻身后现代主义阵营。尽管贝克特的作品至今仍受到很多争议，但他作为20世纪一流文学大师的地位是毫无疑问的。英国有学者如是评价：“就贝克特而言，他的剧作对人生所做的阴暗描绘，我们尽可以不必接受。然而他对于戏剧艺术所做出的贡献却足以赢得我们的感激和尊敬。他描写了人类山穷水尽的苦境，却把戏剧艺术引入了柳暗花明的新村。”

二、剧 情 简 介

《来来往往》（*Come and Go*，1965）是贝克特戏剧作品中一部非常独特的剧作——微型剧（dramaticule）。该剧由3个女主人公并排坐在长凳上展开。舞台上的灯光轮流聚焦在1个女人身上，其余2个被周围的黑暗掩盖，窃窃私语。她们谈论阴暗的光线和“不可见”的好友。舞台上，剧中人在片刻中出现并在长久的黑暗中隐匿交替，最终，她们3人同时出现，像链条般手拉着手。戏剧仅有几十行简短的对话，但有详细的注释解释三人具体的位置变化。该剧以简陋空洞的舞台设计象征意味浓重的舞台人物走位，突破传统的戏剧舞台模式，以短小精悍的形式展现了荒诞派戏剧的形式创新。

三、名篇选读

Come and Go

For John Calder

Written in English early in 1965. First published in French by Editions de Minuit, Paris, in 1966. First published in English by Calder and Boyars, London, in 1967. First produced as Kommen and Gehen, translated by Elmar Tophoven, at the Schiller-Theater Werkstatt, Berlin, on 14 January, 1966. First performed in English at the Peacock Theatre, Dublin, on 28 February, 1968 and subsequently at the Royal Festival Hall, London, on 9 December, 1968.

Characters in the Play

FLO[1]

VI

RU

(Age undeterminable)

(*Sitting centre side by side; stage right to left FLO, VI and RU; Very erect, facing front, hands clasped in laps*)

(*Silence*)

VI: When did we three last meet?

RU: Let us not speak.

(*Silence. Exit VI right. Silence.*)

FLO: Ru.

RU: Yes.

FLO: What do you think of VI?

RU: I see little change. (*FLO moves to centre seat, whispers in RU's ear. Appalled.*) Oh! (They look at each other. FLO puts her finger to her lips.) Does she not realize?

FLO: God grant not.

(*Enter VI. FLO and RU turn back front, resume pose. VI sits right. Silence.*)

Just sit together as we used to, in the playground at Miss Wade's.

RU: On the log.

(*Silence. Exit FLO left. Silence*)

VI: Yes.

RU: How do you find FLO?

VI: She seems much the same. (*RU moves to centre seat, whispers in VI's ear. Appalled.*) Oh! (*They look at each other. RU puts her finger to her lips.*) Has she not been told?

RU: God forbid. (*Enter FLO. RU and VI turn back front, resume pose. FLO sits left.*) Holding hands... that way.

FLO: Dreaming of... love.

(*Silence. Exit RU right. Silence.*)

VI: Flo.

FLO: Yes.

VI: How do you think Ru is looking?

FLO: One sees little in this light. (*VI moves centre seat, whispers in FLO's ear. Appalled.*) Oh! (*They look at each other. VI puts her finger to her lips.*) Does she not know?

VI: Please God not.

(*Enter RU. VI and FLO turn back front, resume pose. RU sits right. Silence.*)

May we not speak of the old days? (Silence) Of what came after? (Silence) Shall we hold hands in the old way?

(*After a moment they join hands as follows: VI's right hand with RU's right hand. VI's left hand with FLO's left hand. FLO's right hand with RU's left hand. VI's arms being above RU's left arm and FLO's right arm. The three pairs of clasped hands rest on the three laps. Silence.)*

FLO: I can feel the rings.

(*Silence*)

CURTAIN

NOTES[2]

Successive positions

1	FLO	VI	RU
2	FLO		RU
		FLO	RU
3	VI	FLO	RU
4	VI		RU
	VI	RU	
5	VI	RU	FLO
6	VI		FLO
		VI	VLO
7	RU	VI	FLO

Hands

RU VI FLO

RU VI FLO

LIGHTING

Soft, from above only and concentrated on playing area. Rest of stage as dark as possible.

COSTUME

Full-length coats, buttoned high, dull violet (RU), dull red (VI), dull yellow (FLO). Drab nondescript hats with enough brim to shade faces. Apart from colour differentiation three figures as alike as possible. Light shoes with rubber soles. Hands made up to be as visible as possible. No rings apparent.

SEAT

Narrow benchlike seat, without back, just long enough to accommodate three figures almost touching. As little visible as possible. It should not be clear what they are sitting on.

EXITS

The figures are not seen to go off stage. They should disappear a few steps from lit area. If dark not sufficient to allow this, recourse should be had to screens or drapes as little visible as possible. Exits and entrances slow, without sound of feet.

OBS

Three very different sounds.

VOICES

As low as compatible with audibility. Colourless except for three 'Ohs' and two lines following.

注释

1. **FLO, VI and RU:** 本剧的三位女性角色。剧本内容极其简短，人物语言简单，但语义跳跃性强，展现了荒诞派戏剧的特点和贝克特的语言风格。
2. 本剧虽然布景简单，但作家从演员的顺序和位置、灯光、服装到道具安排和声音效果均给予了极为详细的舞台说明。

四、拓展思考

1. Beckett clearly states in his notes to the play that "Hands made up to be as visible as possible. No rings apparent." So what are the nonexistent things Flo refers to?
2. Some people think that *Come and Go* means birth and death. When the three women clasp hands at the end, the unbroken chain they form becomes an ironic emblem of eternity. Do you agree? Please state your understating and interpretation.
3. In the play you may notice the absence of Irishness, which has been a core consciousness to the Irish playwrights in the 20th century. How do you understand the absence?

五、延展阅读

贝克特是荒诞派戏剧的代表作家，同时又是新小说的重要作家。他的主要作品都是先以法文写成，所以他也算是一位法国作家。他的剧作充满荒诞感，偏重于表现人们处境的紧迫和精神危机。人物是荒诞的写照，舞台布景则是表现荒诞人物的工具。他的剧中人物通常是流浪汉、乞丐、奴隶等社会小人物，既有着可怜的遭遇，又无比清醒。他们从自身的贫困处境出发，悲观地审视世界，无情地观察自己的命运，并不断思考身份、生存及未来生活等问题。剧中常用荒凉、破旧、废弃的舞台布景来象征空虚、毫无意义的世界。剧中的时间、地点也都被淡化，过去、现在和将来都是荒诞的概念。

贝克特也是新小说的实践者。在《穆尔菲》《莫鲁瓦》和《马洛纳之死》等小说中，他从不同的视角刻画现实的荒诞，突显的是等待、孤独、异化、衰弱、死亡和无法交流等主题，从而隐喻人类的生存危机。他选取的小说人物与其戏剧人物一样，都经历了可怕的遭遇和悲惨的处境。他们是受苦人类的象征。无序、混乱的语言也是他小说的一大特色。有些语句之间缺乏逻辑联系，有些语句前后矛盾、跳跃性强，字句与情节结构多有重复。文本中的标点符号时常被取消，人物对白如同梦中呓语。此外，贝克特还常用文字游戏、双关语等叙述手法。这些创作特点对后来的新小说作家具有很大影响。

CHAPTER 8

肖恩·奥卡西

Sean O'Casey

《朱诺与孔雀》

Juno and the Paycock

一、剧作家简介

肖恩·奥卡西（Sean O' Casey）1880年3月30日出生于都柏林一个贫穷的新教徒家庭，是家中13个孩子中最小的一个。他幼年丧父，从小因患眼疾而失学，直到青春期之前他未曾接受过学校教育。他曾在都柏林铁路工厂做工九年，参加过工人运动及1916年爱尔兰公民军发动的复活节起义。1918年，奥卡西开始创作剧本。

奥卡西的作品以描写战争和革命时期的都柏林贫民窟的现实主义悲喜剧而闻名，在爱尔兰文艺复兴中占重要地位。以都柏林为背景的三部曲《枪手的影子》（*The Shadow of a Gunman*，1923）、《朱诺与孔雀》（*Juno and the Paycock*，1924）、《犁与星》（*The Plough and the Stars*，1926）被认为是他的代表作。奥卡西以现实主义风格聚焦城市生活及贫困生活背景下的非英雄人物。与以往爱尔兰戏剧舞台上塑造的睿智农民的形象不同，奥卡西笔下的这些城市普通人既有性格的可爱之处同时又是具有道德缺陷的人。正是这一打破爱尔兰文艺复兴时期“爱尔兰人”传统的群像塑造手法，使奥卡西的戏剧在上演之初常招致爱尔兰民族主义观众的抗议和批评。

如今，奥卡西的戏剧成就已被充分认可，“一个来自工人阶级的粗犷的天才”终于成为了爱尔兰戏剧舞台杰出的剧作家代表。他和约翰·米林顿·辛格（J. M. Synge，1871—1909）一起被赞为20世纪上半叶爱尔兰民族戏剧发展道路上的扛鼎作家。

1964年9月18日，奥卡西在英国德文郡逝世。

二、剧情简介

《朱诺和孔雀》（*Juno and the Paycock*，1924）以杰克·波伊尔一家为视点，再现了爱尔兰自由邦成立后内战时期城市劳工阶层的矛盾和混乱。波伊尔先生是个爱吹牛、酗酒的闲人，被人称为“孔雀”，他的家庭全靠妻子朱诺照料。一天，波伊尔一家突然被告之将要继承远方亲戚的一笔遗产，这无疑给贫困的家庭带来福音。于是，他们预支了遗产的费用，开始挥霍起来。然而，遗嘱之事最终不过是一场骗局。最后，女儿玛丽被人始乱终弃，在内战中残疾了的儿子约翰也因“出卖”同志被处死。剧尾，“孔雀”依旧陷入酗酒之中，母亲朱诺承担起照顾怀孕的玛丽的责任，代表了家庭不倒的支撑力量。

该剧人物刻画形象生动。大智大勇的母亲朱诺与其醉态百出、自吹自擂的丈夫“孔雀”杰克·波伊尔形成鲜明对比。此外，朱诺与古罗马神话故事及天后朱诺形象形成典故关联，从而赋予了母亲这一形象强烈的传统文化象征意义。

就艺术形式而言，该剧属于典型的现实主义风格。它形象地再现了爱尔兰20世纪20年代的社会现实——困顿的经济、紧张的劳资矛盾和内战时期的混乱政局。但该剧的悲喜剧形式、城市方音和语言风格也值得读者细心品味，并体验奥卡西戏剧艺术的独特魅力。

三、名篇选读

Juno and the Paycock

ACT III

(*MRS. BOYLE enters. It is apparent from the serious look on her face that something has happened. She takes off her hat and coat without a word and puts them by. She then sits down near the fire, and there is a few moments' pause.*)

BOYLE: Well, what did the doctor say about Mary?

MRS. BOYLE: (*in an earnest manner and with suppressed agitation*) Sit down here, Jack. I've something to say to you... about Mary.

BOYLE: (*awed by her manner*) About... Mary?

MRS. BOYLE: Close that door there and sit down here.

BOYLE: (*closing the door*) More throuble[1] in our native land, is it? (*He sits down.*) Well, what is it?

MRS. BOYLE: It's about Mary.

BOYLE: Well, what about Mary—there's nothin'[2] wrong with her, is there?

MRS. BOYLE: I'm sorry to say there's a gradle wrong with her.

BOYLE: A gradle wrong with her! (*peevishly*) First Johnny an'[3] now Mary; is the whole house goin'[4] to become an hospital! It's not consumption,

	is it?
MRS. BOYLE:	No... It's not consumption... It's worse.
JOHNNY:	Worse! Well, we'll have to get her into some place over this. There's no one here to mind her.
MRS. BOYLE:	We'll all have to mind her now. You might as well know now, Johnny, as another time. (*to BOYLE*) D'ye[5] know what the doctor said to me about her, Jack?
BOYLE:	How ud[6] I know—I wasn't there, was I?
MRS. BOYLE:	He tole me to get her married at wanst[7].
BOYLE:	Married at wanst! An' why did he say the like o'[8] that?
MRS. BOYLE:	Because Mary's goin' to have a baby in a short time.
BOYLE:	Goin' to have a baby! —my God, what'll Bentham say when he hears that?
MRS. BOYLE:	Are you blind, man, that you can't see that it was Bentham that has done this wrong to her?[9]
BOYLE:	(*passionately*) Then he'll marry her; he'll have to marry her!
MRS. BOYLE:	You know he's gone to England, an' God knows where he is now.
BOYLE:	I'll folly him; I'll folly him, an' bring him back, an' make him do her justice. The scoundrel, I might ha' known[10] what he was, with his yogees an' his prawna![11]
MRS. BOYLE:	We'll have to keep it quiet till we see what we can do.
BOYLE:	Oh, isn't this a nice thing to come on top o' me, an' the state I'm in! A pretty show I'll be to Joxer an' to that oul' wan[12], Madigan! Amn't I afther[13] goin' through enough without havin'[14] to go through this!
MRS. BOYLE:	What you an' I'll have to go through'll be nothin' to what poor Mary'll have to go through; for you an' me is middlin'[15] old, an' most of our years is spent; but Mary' ll have maybe forty years to face an' handle, an' every wan of them'll be tainted[16] with a bitther[17] memory.
BOYLE:	Where is she? Where is she till I tell her off? I'm tellin' you when I'm done with her she'll be a sorry girl!

MRS. BOYLE: I left her in me sister's till I came to speak to you. You'll say nothin' to her, Jack; ever since she left school she's earned her livin', an' your fatherly care never throubled the poor girl.

BOYLE: Gwan, take her part agen her father! But I'll let you see whether I'll say nothin' to her or no! Her an' her readin'! That's more o' th' blasted nonsense that has the house fallin' down on top of us! What did th' likes of her, born in a tenement house, want with readin'? Her readin's afther bringin' her to a nice pass—oh, it's madnin', madnin', madnin'!

MRS. BOYLE: When she comes back say nothin' to her, Jack, or she'll leave this place.

BOYLE: Leave this place! Ay, she'll leave this place, an' quick too!

MRS. BOYLE: If Mary goes, I'll go with her.

BOYLE: Well, go with her! Well, go, th' pair o' yous! I lived before I seen yous, an' I can live when yous are gone. Isn't this a nice thing to come rollin' in on top o' me afther all your prayin' to St Anthony an' The Little Flower! An' she's a Child o' Mary, too—I wonder what'll the nuns think of her now? An' it'll be bellows'd all over th' disthrict before you could say Jack Robinson; an' whenever I'm seen they'll whisper, 'That's th' father of Mary Boyle that had th' kid be th' swank she used to go with; d'ye know; d'ye know?' To be sure they'll know—more about it than I will meself!

JOHNNY: She should be dhriven[18] out o' th' house she's brought disgrace on!

MRS. BOYLE: Hush, you, Johnny. We needn't let it be bellows'd all over the place; all we've got to do is to leave this place quietly an' go somewhere we're not known, an' nobody'll be th' wiser.

BOYLE: You're talkin' like a two-year-oul' woman. Where'll we get a place ou' o' this? —places aren't that easily got.

MRS. BOYLE: But, Jack, when we get the money...

BOYLE: Money—what money?

MRS. BOYLE: Why, oul' Ellison's money, of course.

BOYLE: There's no money comin' from oul' Ellison, or any one else. Since you've heard of wan throuble, you might as well hear of another. There's no money comin' to us at all—the Will's a wash-out[19]!

MRS. BOYLE: What are you sayin', man—no money?

JOHNNY: How could it be a wash-out?

BOYLE: The boyo[20] that's afther doin' it to Mary done it to me as well. The thick made out the Will wrong; he said in th' Will, only first cousin an' second cousin, instead of mentionin' our names, an' now any one that thinks he's a first cousin or second cousin t'oul' Ellison can claim the money as well as me, an' they're springin' up in hundreds, an' comin' from America an' Australia, thinkin' to get their whack out of it, while all the time the lawyers is gobblin' it u, till there's not as much as ud buy a stockin' for your lovely daughter's baby!

MRS. BOYLE: I don't believe it. I don't believe it. I don't believe it!

JOHNNY: Why did you say nothin' about this before?

MRS. BOYLE: You're not serious, Jack; you're not serious!

BOYLE: I'm tellin' you the scholar, Bentham, made a banjax o' th' Will; instead o' sayin'; 'th' rest o' me property to be divided between me first cousin, Jack Boyle, an' me second cousin, Mick Finnegan, o' Santhry', he writ down only; 'me first an' second cousins', an' the world an' his wife are afther th' property now.

MRS. BOYLE: Now I know why Bentham left poor Mary in th' lurch; I can see it all now—oh, is there not even a middlin' honest man left in th' world?

JOHNNY: (*to BOYLE*) An' you let us run into debt, an' you borreyed[21] money from everybody to fill yourself with beer! An' now you tell us the whole thing's a wash-out! Oh, if it's thrue, I'm done with you, for you're worse than me sisther Mary!

BOYLE: You hole your tongue, d'ye hear? I'll not take any lip from you. Go an' get Bentham if you want satisfaction for all that's afther happenin' us.

JOHNNY: I won't hole me tongue. I won't hole me tongue! I'll tell you what I think of you; father an' all as you are... you...

MRS. BOYLE: Johnny, Johnny, Johnny, for God's sake, be quiet!

JOHNNY: I'll not be quiet. I'll not be quiet; he's a nice father, isn't he? Is it any wondher Mary went asthray, when...

MRS. BOYLE: Johnny, Johnny, for my sake be quiet—for your mother's sake!

BOYLE: I'm goin' out now to have a few dhrinks with th' last few makes I have, an' tell that lassie o' yours not to be here when I come back; for if I lay me eyes on her, I'll lay me hans on her, an' if I lay me hans on her, I won't be accountable for me actions!

JOHNNY: Take care somebody doesn't lay his hands on you—y'oul'...

MRS. BOYLE: Johnny, Johnny!

BOYLE: (*at door, about to go out*) Oh, a nice son, an' a nicer daughter, I have. (*calling loudly upstairs*) Joxer, Joxer, are you there?

JOXER: (*from a distance*) I'm here. More... ee... aar... i... tee!

BOYLE: I'm goin' down to Foley's—are you comin'?

JOXER: Come with you? With that sweet call me heart is stirred; I'm only waiting for the word, an' I'll be with you, like a bird!

(*BOYLE and JOXER pass the door going out.*)

JOHNNY: (*throwing himself on the bed*) I've a nice sister, an' a nice father; there's no bettin' on it. I wish to God a bullet or a bomb had whipped me ou' o' this long ago! Not one o' yous, not one o' yous have any thought for me!

MRS. BOYLE: (*with passionate remonstrance*) If you don't whisht, Johnny, you'll drive me mad. Who has kep' th' home together for the past few years—only me? An' who'll have to bear th' biggest part o' this throuble but me? —but whinin' an' whingin' isn't goin' to do any good.

JOHNNY: You're to blame yourself for a gradle of it—givin' him his own way in everything, an' never assin' to check him; no matther what he done. Why didn't you look afther th' money? Why...

(*There is a knock at the door. MRS BOYLE opens it. JOHNNY rises on his elbow to look and listen; two men enter.*)

FIRST MAN: We've been sent up be th' Manager of the Hibernian Furnishing Co., Mrs Boyle, to take back the furniture that was got a while ago.

MRS. BOYLE: Yous'll touch nothin' here—how do I know who yous are?

FIRST MAN: (*showing a paper*) There's the ordher, ma'am. (*reading*) A chest o' drawers, a table, wan easy an' two ordinary chairs, wan mirror, wan chestherfield divan, an' a wardrobe an' two vases. (*to his comrade*) Come on, Bill, it's afther knockin'-off time already.

JOHNNY: For God's sake, mother, run down to Foley's an' bring father back, or we'll be left without a stick.

(*The men carry out the table.*)

MRS. BOYLE: What good would it be? —you heard what he said before he went out.

JOHNNY: Can't you thry? He ought to be here, an' the like of this goin' on.

(*MRS BOYLE puts a shawl around her, as Mary enters.*)

MARY: What's up, mother? I met men carryin' away the table, an' everybody's talking about us not gettin' the money after all.

MRS. BOYLE: Everythin's gone wrong, Mary, everythin'. We're not gettin' a penny out o' the Will, not a penny— I'll tell you all when I come back. I'm goin' for your father. (*She runs out.*)

JOHNNY: (*to MARY, who has sat down by the fire*) It's a wondher you're not ashamed to show your face here, afther what has happened.

(*JERRY enters slowly; there is a look of earnest hope on his face. He looks at MARY for a few moments.*)

JERRY: (*softly*) Marry!

(*MARY does not answer.*)

Mary, I want to speak to you for a few moments, may I?

(*MARY remains silent. JOHNNY goes slowly into room on left.*)

Your mother has told me everything, Mary, and I have come to you... I have come to tell you, Mary, that my love for you is greater and deeper than ever...

MARY: (*with a sob*) Oh, Jerry, Jerry, say no more; all that is over now; anything like that is impossible now!

JERRY: Impossible? Why do you talk like that, Mary?

MARY: After all that has happened.

JERRY: What does it matter what has happened? We are young enough to be able to forget all those things. (*He catches her hand.*) Mary, Mary, I am pleading for your love. With Labour, Mary, humanity is above everything; we are the Leaders in the fight for a new life. I want to forget Bentham. I want to forget that you left me—even for a while.

MARY: Oh, Jerry, Jerry, you haven't the bitter word of scorn for me after all.

JERRY: (*passionately*) Scorn! I love you, love you, Mary!

MARY: (*rising, and looking him in the eyes*) Even though...

JERRY: Even though you threw me over for another man; even though you gave me many a bitter word!

MARY: Yes, yes, I know; but you love me, even though... even though... I'm... goin'... goin'...

(*He looks at her questioningly, and fear gathers in his eyes.*)

Ah, I was thinkin' so... You don't know everything!

JERRY: (*poignantly*) Surely to God, Mary, you don't mean that... that... that...

MARY: Now you know all, Jerry; now you know all!

JERRY: My God, Mary, have you fallen as low as that?

MARY: Yes, Jerry, as you say, I have fallen as low as that.

JERRY: I didn't mean it that way. Mary... it came on me so sudden, that I didn't mind that I was sayin'... I never expected this—your mother never told me... I'm sorry... God knows, I'm sorry for you, Mary.

MARY: Let us say no more, Jerry. I don't blame you for thinkin' it's terrible... I suppose it is... Everybody'll think the same... it's only as I expected—your humanity is just as narrow as the humanity of the others.

JERRY: I'm sorry, all the same... I shouldn't have troubled you... I wouldn't if I'd known... If I can do anything for you... Mary... I will. (*He turns to go, and halts at the door.*)

MARY: Do you remember, Jerry, the verses you read when you gave the lecture in the Socialist Rooms some time ago, on Humanity's Strife with Nature?

JERRY: The verses—no. I don't remember them.

MARY: I do. They're runnin' in me head now—
An' we felt the power that fashion'd
All the lovely things we saw,
That created all the murmur
Of an everlasting law,
Was a hand of force an' beauty
With an eagle's tearin' claw;
Then we saw our globe of beauty
Was an ugly thing as well;
A hymn divine whose chorus
Was an agonizin' yell
Like the story of a demon;
That an angel had to tell
Like a glowin' picture by a
Hand unsteady, brought to ruin;
Like her craters, if their deadness
Could give life unto the moon;
Like the agonizing horror
Of a violin out of tune.

(*There is a pause, and DEVINE goes slowly out.*)

JOHNNY: (*returning*) Is he gone?

MARY: Yes.

(*The two men re-enter.*)

FIRST MAN: We can't wait any longer for t'oul' fella—sorry, Miss, but we have to live as well as th' nex' man.

(*They carry out some things.*)

JOHNNY: Oh, isn't this terrible!... I suppose you told him everything... couldn't you have waited for a few days? ...he'd have stopped th' takin' of the things, if you'd kep' your mouth shut. Are you burnin' to tell every one of the shame you've brought on us?

MARY: (*snatching up her hat and coat*) Oh, this is unbearable! (*She rushes out.*)

FIRST MAN: (*re-entering*) We'll take the chest o' drawers next—it's the heaviest.

(*The votive light*[22] *flickers for a moment, and goes out.*)

JOHNNY: (*in a cry of fear*) Mother o' God, the light's afther goin' out!

FIRST MAN: You put the win'up me the way you bawled that time. The oil's all gone, that's all.

JOHNNY: (*with an agonizing cry*) Mother o' God, there's a shot I'm afther gettin'!

FIRST MAN: What's wrong with you, man? Is it a fit you're takin'?

JOHNNY: I'm afther feelin' a pain in me breast, like the tearin' by of a bullet!

FIRST MAN: He's goin' mad—it's a wondher they'd leave a chap like that here by himself.

(*Two Irregulars enter swiftly; they carry revolvers; one goes over to Johnny; the other covers the two furniture men.*)

FIRST IRREGULAR: (*to the men, quietly and incisively*) Who are you? —what are you doin' here? —quick!

FIRST MAN: Removin' furniture that's not paid for.

FIRST IRREGULAR: Get over to the other end of the room an' turn your faces to the wall—quick!

(*The two men turn their faces to the wall, with their hands up.*)

SECOND IRREGULAR: (*to JOHNNY*) Come on, Sean Boyle, you're wanted; some of us have a word to say to you.

JOHNNY: I'm sick, I can't—what do you want with me?

SECOND IRREGULAR: Come on, come on; we've a distance to go, an' haven't much time—come on.

JOHNNY: I'm an oul' comrade—yous wouldn't shoot an oul' comrade.

SECOND IRREGULAR: Poor Tancred[23] was an oul' commrade o'yours, but you didn't think o' that when you gave him away to the gang that sent him to his grave. But we've no time to waste; come on—here, Dermot, ketch his arm. (*to JOHNNY*) Have you your beads?

JOHNNY: Me beads? Why do you ass me that, why do you ass me that?

SECOND IRREGULAR: Go on, go on, march!

JOHNNY: Are yous goin' to do in a comrade? —look at me arm, I lost it for Ireland.

SECOND IRREGULAR: Commandant Tancred lost his life for I reland.

JOHNNY: Sacred Hearts of Jesus have mercy on me! Mother o' God, pray for me—be with me now in the agonies o' death!... Hail, Mary, full o'grace... the Lord is... with Thee.

(*They drag out JOHNNY BOYLE, and the curtain falls.*)

注释

1. **throuble:** 都柏林方言，即英语trouble。
2. **nothin':** 都柏林方言，即英语nothing。
3. **an':** 都柏林方言，即英语and。
4. **goin':** 都柏林方言，即英语going。
5. **d'ye:** 都柏林方言，即英语do you。
6. **ud:** 都柏林方言，即英语would。
7. **at wanst:** 都柏林方言，即英语at once。
8. **O':** 都柏林方言，即英语of。
9. **has done this wrong to her:** 指边沁（Bentham）使玛丽怀孕一事。
10. **ha' known:** 都柏林方言，即英语have known。
11. **yogees an' his prawna!:** 指边沁和波伊尔家人聚会时提及的信念。
12. **oul' wan:** 都柏林方言，即英语old one。
13. **afther:** 都柏林方言，即英语after。
14. **havin':** 都柏林方言，即英语having。
15. **middlin':** 都柏林方言，即英语middle。
16. **tainted:** 污染的，感染的。
17. **bitther:** 都柏林方言，即英语bitter。
18. **dhriven:** 都柏林方言，即英语drive。
19. **the Will's a wash-out:** 都柏林方言，即英语the will turns out to be a cheat。

20. **boyo:** 指前文中提及的边沁。
21. **borreyed:** 都柏林方言，即英语borrowed。
22. **The votive light:** 约翰尼将其看作是自己生命的象征。
23. **Tancred:** 约翰尼的挚友和同志，后因约翰尼的背叛死于一场罢工中。

四、拓展思考

1. How do you understand the maternal image of "Juno" in the play? What is the intertextual relationship between the mother "Juno" and the Heaven Queen of "Juno" in the ancient Roman myth?
2. How dose the death of John reflect the great disaster brought by the Irish civil war in the 1920s? What political attitude from the playwright may be viewed through the typical family tragedy?
3. How do the family members respond to the news that Mary gets pregnant? Through the males' attitude towards the affair, what kind of social position of women may be judged under the traditional Catholic culture at that moment?

五、延展阅读

肖恩·奥卡西是继辛格之后爱尔兰著名的现实主义戏剧家。在他童年时期，家庭生活的贫苦和母亲的辛劳操持为他日后的创作提供了丰富的素材。这就是其剧本中“贫民窟现实主义”（slum realism）特征和勇敢、能干的母亲形象。

奥卡西早期佳作“都柏林三部曲”（《枪手的影子》《朱诺与孔雀》和《犁与星》）是他剧作成就的顶峰。这三部剧本都曾在阿贝剧院上演，并都是以爱尔兰民族独立运动时期都柏林的贫民区为背景，反映了1920年发生的爱尔兰独立运动和英国镇压过程中的暴力、恐怖和对普通百姓的影响。

在反思爱尔兰民族性格这一层面上，辛格运用的是爱尔兰农民生活和民间传说，而奥卡西则选取都市中下层市民的生活。他的“都柏林三部曲”都是悲剧，但却融入了喜剧和闹剧的特点，使作品节奏张弛有度，既有悲剧效果又有反讽意味。更重要的是，奥卡西通过“三部曲”深刻地反映了独立运动时期的市民心态和独立运动所面临的矛盾与问题，体现了一个作家对民族命运的深层关注。

CHAPTER 9

布莱恩·弗里尔

Brian Friel

《卢纳莎之舞》

Dancing at Lughnasa

一、剧作家简介

布莱恩·弗里尔（Brian Friel）是当代爱尔兰剧坛最具影响力、最具国际声誉的剧作家之一。弗里尔一生笔耕不缀。从1962年到2008年，弗里尔先后完成了32个剧本，其中原创戏剧24部，根据他人作品改编的戏剧8部。其中，1964年的《费城，我来了》（*Philadelphia Here I Come*）标志着当代爱尔兰戏剧时代的到来，其后不同历史时期的代表性剧作如《心理救助者》（*Faith Healer*，1979）、《翻译》（*Translations*，1980）、《创造历史》（*Making History*，1988)、《卢纳莎之舞》（*Dancing at Lughnasa*，1990）以不断更新的戏剧艺术深刻记录了20世纪下半叶爱尔兰的社会生活状态。

弗里尔立足于爱尔兰本土，专注戏剧创作，赢得了高度的国际认同和赞誉。除剧作频频获得国际戏剧奖项外，弗里尔还凭借其卓越的戏剧成就和影响力成为了“美国文学与艺术院荣誉院士”（American Academy of Arts and Letters）和“英国皇家文学协会成员”（A Fellow of Royal Society of Literature）。

90年代，弗里尔成为当代爱尔兰戏剧的标杆性人物。1990年，著名的戏剧评论家潘（Richard Pine）在其专著《弗里尔与爱尔兰戏剧》（*Brian Friel and Contemporary Irish Drama*）里首次将弗里尔及其《费城，我来了》确定为当代爱尔兰戏剧的分水岭，引发戏剧史界的热议。1998年，弗里尔的戏剧《卢纳莎之舞》被改编成电影，搬上大银屏，弗里尔的名字也因此成为剧场和影院的票房保证。爱尔兰剧坛和戏剧评论界丝毫不吝啬对他的崇高礼遇。1999年适逢弗里尔70大寿，都柏林戏剧节当年上演的所有剧目均是弗里尔的作品；2009年又值弗里尔80华诞，一系列学术杂志和学术会议均以弗里尔为专题。北爱尔兰女王大学还建立了以弗里尔名字命名的剧院（Brain Friel Theatre）。到新世纪的第一个十年末，弗里尔被完全经典化，其戏剧地位被深固在当代爱尔兰戏剧史册上。

二、剧情简介

《卢纳莎之舞》讲述了1936年夏天发生在芒迪家庭（Mundy Family）的一系列变化。

芒迪五姐妹带着最小的妹妹克里斯蒂娜（Christina）的非婚子、7岁的迈克一起，生活贫困却很平静。大姐凯特（Kate）是中学教师，支撑着家里主要生活来源；二姐艾格尼丝（Agnes）和小妹罗斯（Rose）靠出售在家编织的手工织品贴补家用；曼吉（Maggie）和迈克妈妈克里斯蒂娜承担家务。

但是，这种平静的生活很快被打破。大哥杰克神父（Father Jack）结束了在非洲25年的传教生活，被“不体面地”遣送回乡，笃信天主教的凯特因此丢了教职。村子里进驻了工厂，艾格尼丝和罗斯的家庭作坊受到冲击，手工织品无法再售出，家庭经济几经瘫痪。在物质和精神的双重困顿之中，支撑着芒迪姐妹的是无线电收音机的音乐和在后花园跳的古凯尔特卢纳莎舞蹈。她们以舞蹈的形式抒发内心的苦痛，寻求精神的慰藉。

本剧的内涵十分丰富。剧中卢纳莎节和卢纳莎舞蹈所代表的古凯尔特文化、杰克对非洲异教文化的迷恋、工业化对于传统乡村生活的冲击等都能引发读者多层次和多角度的思考。

全剧由两幕组成。本节选自第一幕，以回忆剧的形式透过成年迈克的回忆再现了1936年夏天的经历。回忆剧的不可靠叙述体现了该剧形式特色。

三、名篇选读

Dancing at Lughnasa

ACT I

Characters in the Play

Michael, a young man, the narrator

Kate, forty, a school teacher

Maggie, thirty-eight, housekeeper

Agnes, thirty-five, knitter

Rose, thirty-two, knitter

Chris, twenty-six, Michael's mother

Gerry, thirty-three, Michael's father

Jack, fifty-three, missionary priest

Michael, who narrates the story, also speaks the lines of the boy, i.e. himself when he was seven.

ACT I: *A warm day in early August, 1936.*

The home of the Mundy family, two miles outside the village of Ballybeg, County Donegal, Ireland.

SET: *Slightly more than half the area of the stage is taken up by the kitchen on the right (left and right from the point of view of the audience). The rest of the stage—i.e. the remaining area stage left—is the garden adjoining the house. The garden is neat but not cultivated.*

Upstage centre is a garden seat.

The (unseen) boy has been making two kites in the garden and pieces of wood, paper, cord, etc., are lying on the ground close to the garden seat. One kite is almost complete.

There are two doors leading out of the kitchen. The front door leads to the garden and the front of the house. The second in the top right-hand corner leads to the bedrooms and the area behind the house.

One kitchen window looks out front. A second window looks on to the garden.

There is a sycamore tree off right. One of its branches reaches over part of the house.

The room has the furnishings of the usual country kitchen of the thirties: a large iron range, a large turf box beside it, table and chairs, dresser, oil lamp, buckets with water at the back door, etc. But because this is the home if the five women the austerity of the furnishings is relived by some gracious touches-flowers, pretty curtains, an attractive dresser arrangement, etc.

DRESS: *Kate, the teacher, is the only wage-earner. Agnes and Rose make a little money knitting gloves at home. Chris and Maggie have no income. So the clothes of all the sisters reflect their lean circumstances. Rose wears wellingtons even though the day is warm. Maggie wears large boots with long, unites laces. Rose, Maggie and Agnes all wear the drab, wrap-around overall/aprons of the time.*

In the opening tableau Father Jack is wearing the uniform of a British army officer chaplain—a magnificent and immaculate uniform of dazzling white, gold epaulettes and gold buttons, tropical hat, clerical collar, military cane. He stands stiffly to attention. As the text says, he is 'resplendent', 'magnificent', so resplendent that he looks almost comic opera.

In this tableau, too, Gerry is wearing a spotless white tricorn hat with splendid white plumage. (Soiled and shabby versions of Jack's uniform and Gerry's ceremonial hat are worn at the end of the play, i.e. in the final tableau.)

Rose is 'simple'. All her sisters are kind to her and protective of her. But Agnes has taken on the role of special protector.

When the play opens, Michael is standing downstage left in a pool of light. The rest of the stage is in darkness. Immediately Michael begins speaking, slowly being up the lights on the rest of the stage.

Around the stage and at a distance from Michael, the other characters stand motionless in formal tableau. Maggie is at the kitchen window (right). Chris is at the front door. Kate is at extreme stage right. Rose and Gerry sit on the garden seat. Jack stands beside Rose. Agnes is upstage left. They hold these positions while Michael talks to the audience.

MICHAEL: When I cast my mind back to that summer of 1936 different kinds of memories offer themselves to me. We got our first wireless set[1] that summer—well, a sort of a set, and it obsessed us. And because it arrived as August the First was Lughnasa[2], the feast day of the pagan god Lugh, and the days and weeks of harvesting that followed were called the Festival of Lughnasa. But Aunt Kate—she was a national school teacher and a very proper woman[3]—she with any kind of name, not to talk of a pagan god. So we just called it Marconi[4] because that was a pagan god. So we just called it Marconi because that was the name emblazoned on the set.

And about three weeks before we got that wireless, my mother's brother, my Uncle Jack, came home from Africa for the first time ever. For twenty-five years he had worked in a leper colony there, in a remote village called Ryanga in Uganda. The only time he ever left that village was for about six months during the World War One when he as chaplain to the British arm in East Africa. Then back for a further eighteen years. And now in his early fifties and in bad health he had come to home to Ballybeg—as it turned out—to die.

And when I cast mind back to that summer of 1936, these two memories—of our first wireless and of Father Jack's return—are always linked. So that when I recall my first shock at Jack's appearance, shrunken and jaundiced with malaria. At the same time I remember my first delight, indeed my awe, at the sheer magic of that radio. And when I remember the kitchen throbbing with the beat of Irish dance music beamed to us all the way from Athlone[5], and my mother and her sisters suddenly catching hands and dancing a spontaneous step-dance and laughing—screaming! —like excited schoolgirls at the same time I see that forlorn figure of Father Jack shuffling from room to room as if he were searching for something but couldn't remember what. And even through I was only a child of seven at the time I know I had a sense of unease, some awareness of a widening breach between what seemed to be and what was, of things changing too quickly before my eyes, of becoming what they ought to be. That may have been because Uncle Jack hadn't turned out at all like the resplendent figure in my head. Or maybe because I had witnessed Marconi's voodoo[6] derange those kind, sensible women and transform them into shrieking strangers. Or maybe it was because during those Lughnasa weeks of 1936 we were visited on two occasions by my father, Gerry Even, and for the first time in my life I had a chance to observe them.

(*The lights changes. The kitchen and garden are now lit as for a warm summer afternoon.*

Michael, Kate, Gerry and Father Jack go off. The others busy themselves with their tasks. Maggie makes a mash for hens. Agnes knits gloves. Rose carries a basket of turf into kitchen and empties it into the large box beside the range. Chris irons at the kitchen table. They all work in silence. Then Chris stops ironing, goes to the tiny mirror on the wall and scrutinizes her face.)

CHRIS:	When we are going to get a decent mirror to see ourselves in?
MAGGIE:	You can see enough to do you.
CHRIS:	I'm going to throw this aul cracked thing out.
MAGGIE:	Indeed you're not, Chrissie. I'm the one that broke it and the only way to avoid seven year's luck[7] is to keep on using it.
CHRIS:	You can see nothing in it.
AGNES:	Except more and more wrinkles.
CHRIS:	D'you know what I think I might do? I think I just might start wearing lipsticks.
AGNES:	Do you hear this, Maggie?
MAGGIE:	Steady on, girl. Today it's lipstick; tomorrow it's the gin bottle.
CHRIS:	I think I just might.
AGNES:	As long as Kate's not around. 'Do you want to make a pagan of yourself?'
	(*Chris puts her face up close to the mirror and feels it.*)
CHRIS:	Far too pale. And the aul mousey hair. Needs a bit of colour.
AGNES:	What for?
CHRIS:	What indeed. (*She shrugs and goes back to her ironing. She holds up a surplice.*) Make a nice dress that, wouldn't it? God forgive me.
	(*Work continues. Nobody speaks. Then suddenly and unexpectedly Rose burst into raucous song.*)
ROSE:	"Will you come to Abyssinia, will you come? Bring your own cup and saucer and a bun..."
	(*As she sings the next two lines she dances—a gauche graceless shuffle that defies the rhythm of the song.*)
	'Mussolini will be there with his airplanes in the air. Will you come to Abyssinia, will you come?'
	Not bad, Maggie—eh?
	(*Maggie is trying to light a very short cigarette butt.*)
MAGGIE:	You should be on the stage, Rose.
	(*Rose continues to shuffle and now holds up her apron skirt.*)

ROSE: And not a bad bit of leg, Maggie-eh?

MAGGIE: Rose Mundy! Where' your modesty! (*Maggie now hitches her own skirt even higher than Rose's and does a similar shuffle.*) Is that not more like it?

ROSE: Good, Maggie-good-good! Look, Agnes, look!

AGNES: A right pair of pagans, the two of you.

ROSE: Turn on Marconi, Chrissie.

CHRIS: I've told you a dozen times: the battery's dead.

ROSE: It is not. It went for me a while ago. (*She goes to the set and switches in on. There is a sudden, loud three-second blast of The British Grenadiers.*) You see! Takes aul Rosie! (*She is about to launch into a dance-and the music suddenly dies.*)

CHRIS: Told you.

ROSE: That aul set's useless.

AGNES: Kate'll have a new battery back with her.

CHRIS: If it's the battery that's wrong.

ROSE: Is Abyssinia in Africa, Aggie?

AGNES: Yes.

ROSE: Is there a war there?

AGNES: Yes, I've told you that.

ROSE: But' that's not where Father Jack was, is it?

AGNES: (*patiently*) Jack was in Uganda, Rosie. That's a different part of Africa. You know that.

ROSE: (*unhappily*) Yes, I do... I do... I know that...

(*Maggie catches her hand and sings softly into her ear to the same melody as the 'Abyssinia' song.*)

MAGGIE: "Will you vote for De Valera[8], will you vote?
If you don't, we'll be like Gandhi[9] with his goat."
(*Rose and Maggie now sing the next two lines together.*)
"Uncle Bill from Baltinglass has a wireless up his—"
(*They dance as they sing the final line of the song.*)

"Will you vote for De Valera, will you vote?"

MAGGIE: I'll tell you something, Rosie; the pair of us should be on the stage.

ROSE: The pair of us should be on the stage, Aggie!

(*They return to their tasks. Agnes goes to the cupboard for wool. On her way back to her seat she looks out the window that looks on to the garden.*)

AGNES: What's that son of yours at our there?

CHRIS: God knows. As long as he's quiet.

AGNES: He's making something. Looks like a kite. (*She taps on the window, calls 'Michael' and blows a kiss to the imaginary child.*) Oh, that was the wrong thing to do! He's going to have your hair, Chris.

CHRIS: Mine's like a whin-bush. Will you wash it for me tonight, Maggie?

MAGGIE: Are we all for a big dance somewhere?

CHRIS: After I've put Michael to bed. What about then?

MAGGIE: I'm your man.

AGNES: (*at window*) Pity there aren't some boys about to play with.

MAGGIE: Now you are talking. Couldn't we all do with that?

AGNES: (*leaving window*) Maggie!

MAGGIE: Wouldn't it be just great if we had a— (*breaks off*) Shhh.

CHRIS: What is it?

MAGGIE: Thought I heard Father Jack at the back door. I hope Kate remembers his quinine.

AGNES: She'll remember. Kate forgets nothing.

(*pause*)

ROSE: There's going to be pictures in the hall next Saturday, Aggie. I think maybe I'll go.

AGNES: (*guarded*) Yes?

ROSE: I might be meeting somebody there.

AGNES: Who's that?

ROSE: I'm not saying.

CHRIS: Do we know him?

ROSE: I'm not saying.

AGNES: You'll enjoy that, Rosie. You loved the last picture we saw.

ROSE: And he wants to bring me up to the back hills next Sunday—up to Lough Anna. His father has a boat there. And I'm thinking maybe I'll bring a bottle of milk with me. And I've enough money saved to buy a packet of chocolate biscuits.

CHRIS: Danny Bradley is a scut, Rose.

ROSE: I never said it was Danny Bradley!

CHRIS: He's a married man with three young children.

ROSE: And that's just where you're wrong, missy—so there! (*to Agnes*) She left him six months ago, Aggie, and went to England.

MAGGIE: Rose, love, we just want—

ROSE: (*to Chris*) And who are you to talk, Christina Mundy! Don't you dare lecture me!

MAGGIE: Everybody in the town knows that Danny Bradley is—

ROSE: (*to Maggie*) And you're jealous, too! That's what's wrong with the whole of you—you're jealous of me! (*to Agnes*) He calls me his Rosebud. He waited for me outside the chapel gate last Christmas morning and he gave me this. (*She opens the front of her apron. A charm and a medal are pinned to her jumper.*) "That's for my Rosebud," he said.

AGNES: Is it a fish, Rosie?

ROSE: Isn't it lovely? It's made for pure silver. And it brings you good luck.

AGNES: It is lovely.

ROSE: I wear it all the time—beside my miraculous medal. (*pause*) I love him, Aggie.

AGNES: I know.

CHRIS: (*softly*) Bastard!

(*Rose closes the front of her apron. She is on the point of tears. Silence. Now Maggie lifts her hen-bucket and using it as a dancing partner; she does a very fast and very exaggerated tango across the kitchen floor as she sings in her parodic style the words from 'The Isle of Capri'.*)

MAGGIE:	'Summer time was nearly over. Blue Italian skies above. I said, "Mister, I'm a rover. Can't you spare a sweet word for love?" (*And without pausing for breath she begins calling her hens as she exists by the back door.*) **Tchook-tchook-tchook-tchook-tchook-tchook-tchook-tchookeeeeeee...** (*Michael enters and stands stage left. Rose takes the lid off the range and throws turf into the fire.*)
CHRIS:	For God's sake, I have an iron in there.
ROSE:	How was I to know that?
CHRIS:	Don't you see me ironing? (*fishing with tongs*) Now you've lost it. Get out of my road, will you?
AGNES:	Rosie, love, would you give me a hand with this (*of wool*)? If we don't work a bit faster we'll never get two dozen pairs finished this week. (*The convention must now be established that the (imaginary) Boy Michael is working at the kite materials lying on the ground. No dialogue with the Boy Michael must ever be addressed directly to adult Michael, the narrator. Here, for example, Maggie has her back to the narrator. Michael responds to Maggie in his ordinary narrator's voice. Maggie enters the garden from the back of the house.*)
MAGGIE:	What are these supposed to be?
BOY:	Kites.
MAGGIE:	Kites! God help your wit!
BOY:	Watch where you're walking, Aunt, Maggie—you're standing on a tail.
MAGGIE:	Did it squeal? —haaaa! I'll make a deal with you, cub. I'll give you a penny if those things ever leave the ground. Right?
BOY:	You're on. (*She now squats down beside him.*)
MAGGIE:	I've new riddles for you.
BOY:	Give up.

MAGGIE: What goes round the house and round the house and it's in the corner? (*pause*) A broom! Why is a river like a watch?

BOY: You're pathetic.

MAGGIE: Because it never goes far without winding! Hairy out and hairy in, lift your foot and stab it in—what is it?

(*pause*)

BOY: Give up.

MAGGIE: Think!

BOY: Give up!

MAGGIE: Have you even one brain in your head?

BOY: Give up.

MAGGIE: A sock!

BOY: A what?

MAGGIE: A sock—a sock! You know—lift your foot and stab it— (*She demonstrates. No response.*) D'you know what your trouble is, cub? You—are buck-stupid!

BOY: Look out—that's a rat!

(*She screams and leaps to her feet in terror.*)

MAGGIE: Where? where? where? Jesus, Mary and Joseph, where is it?

BOY: Caught you again, Aunt Maggie.

MAGGIE: You evil wee brat—God forgive you! I'll get you fir that, Michael! Don't you worry—I won't forget that! (*She picks up her bucket and moves off towards the back of the house. Stops.*) And I had a barley sugar sweet for you.

BOY: Are these bits of cigarette tobacco stuck to it ?

MAGGIE: Jesus Christ! Someday you're going to fill some woman's life full of happiness. (*moving off*) Tchook-tchook-tchook-tchook... (*Again she stops and throws him a sweet.*) There. I hope it chokes you. (*exists*)

MICHAEL: When I saw Uncle Jack for the first time the reason I was so shocked by his appearance was that I expected well, I suppose, the hero from a schoolboy's book. Once I had seen a photograph of him radiant and splendid in his officer's uniform. It had fallen out of Aunt Kate's prayer book and she snatched it from me before I could study it in detail. It was a picture taken in 1917 when he was a chaplain to the British forces in East Africa and he looked magnificent. But Aunt Kate had been involved locally in the War of Independence[10]; so Father Jack's brief career in the British army was never referred to in that house. All the same the wonderful Father Jack of that photo was the image of him that lodged in my mind.

But if he was a hero to me, he was a hero and saint to my mother and to my aunts. They pored over his occasional letters and for the success of his mission. They scraped and saved for him six pence here, a shilling there-sacrifices they made willingly, joyously, so that they would have a little money to send to him at Christmas and for his birthday. And every so often when a story would appear in the Donegal Enquirer about 'our own leper priest', as they called him—because Ballybeg[11] was proud of him, the whole of Donegal[12] was proud of him—it was only natural that our family would enjoy a small share of that fame—it gave us that little bit of status in the eyes of the parish. And it must have helped my aunts to bear the shame Mother brought on the household by having me—as it was called then—our of wedlock.

(Kate enters left, laden with shopping bags. When she sees the Boy working at his kites her face lights up with pleasure. She watches him for a few seconds. Then she goes to him.)

注释

1. **wireless set:** 收音机。
2. **Lughnasa:** 标志着丰收季节开始的凯尔特异教节日。这是爱尔兰在基督教化之前的四大凯尔特节日之一，为纪念凯尔特文化中最重要的神——光与太阳之神（Lugh）而设，人们在庆祝仪式上跳有凯尔特特色的舞蹈。
3. 这里提到的大姐Kate是个得体的女人。她在天主教会创办的学校任教，不同意用异教神祇来命名这台收音机。这里也象征着天主教和异教的一次较量。
4. **Marconi:** 意大利无线电报发明者。

5. **Athlone:** 城市名，位于爱尔兰中部，是爱尔兰的政治、经济与文化中心。
6. **voodoo:** 一种古老的宗教。这里指收音机似乎有魔法，让女人们情绪激动、翩翩起舞，表现了人们对传统文化的热爱。
7. 西方民间有个说法：打破镜子倒霉七年。
8. **De Valera:** 曾任爱尔兰共和国总统，长期坚持反对英国殖民统治的斗争。
9. **Gandhi:** 现代印度国父，倡导“非暴力不合作运动”，主张用和平方式带领国家脱离英国的殖民统治。
10. 爱尔兰独立战争（1919—1921），也称英爱战争。
11. **Ballybeg:** 弗里尔虚构的一个位于爱尔兰西北部Donegal郡的小镇，在爱尔兰语中写作“Baile Beag”，意为“小镇”。作者在这里将之英语化为“Ballybeg”，影射并控诉英国殖民者将每个爱尔兰的地名都英语化的语言暴力行径。
12. **Donegal:** 爱尔兰西北部的一个郡，有着浓厚的爱尔兰文化气息。

四、拓展思考

1. Please analyze the role of such images as wireless set and bike in the play. How do the images relate to the industrialization?
2. Since the play is entitled as *Dancing at Lughnasa*, how do you interpret the role of pagan dance, as representation of Celtic culture? How does the pagan Celtic dance connect with displaced Father Jack?
3. Michael is called by Uncle Jack as “a Love child”. Is the label in accordance with Irish Catholic culture? How does the calling let out Father Jacks’ displacement?

五、延展阅读

弗里尔的戏剧创作跨越了爱尔兰独立（1948年）以来的40年时间——从1960—1990年。这40年是爱尔兰政治、经济发展发生重大变化的重要阶段。这40年见证了爱尔兰的政治和宗教从冲突走向和平的过程，见证了爱尔兰从传统农耕国家转变为以电子工业为龙头的新型现代化国家的过程。在一定程度上，弗里尔继承了叶芝在20世纪初开创的爱尔兰现实主义戏剧传统。在20世纪下半叶，弗里尔通过戏剧创作艺术性地反映了当代爱尔兰的历史进程。弗里尔的戏剧对于爱尔兰文化，如语言问题、身份认同问题都体现出比前辈更为深邃的历史和文化反思性。

作为一名当代剧作家，弗里尔是一个有益的参照点。读者可以纵向将他与叶芝在20世纪初开创的传统文化进行比较，可以更为清晰地整体把握20世纪爱尔兰民族现实主义戏剧传统和深刻的民族文化反思价值。弗里尔又不仅仅是一名作家，他对于当代爱尔兰的戏剧贡献还在于和爱尔兰演员（Rea）在80年代初共同创建了户外日戏剧公司（Field Day Theatre Company）。该公司以弗里尔的家乡德里（这里还孕育了1995年诺贝尔文学奖得主谢默斯·希尼、当代爱尔兰文学评论家谢默斯·迪恩）为戏剧总部，每年推出一部大戏，在全国不断巡演。由于弗里尔的号召力，户外日戏剧公司吸引了诗人希尼（Seamus Heaney，1939—2013）和文学评论家特里·伊格尔顿（Terry Eagleton）为公司创作剧本，如希尼的《特洛伊的弥合》（*Cure at Troy*，1990）、伊格尔顿的《圣人王尔德》（*Saint Wilde*，1989）。1980—1992年是户外日戏剧公司的“黄金十二年”，在该舞台上演的十二部大戏成为20世纪后半叶爱尔兰文坛上一道亮丽的文学风景。

CHAPTER 10

玛丽娜·卡尔

Marina Carr

《猫原边……》

By the Bog of Cats...

一、剧作家简介

玛丽娜·卡尔（Marina Carr）1964年出生于都柏林，在爱尔兰中部的奥发利郡长大。荒凉的奥发利郡成为卡尔作品的重要标识。1983年，卡尔进入爱尔兰都柏林大学攻读英语和哲学。在大学期间，卡尔开始展现出戏剧天赋，并创作了首部戏剧。

卡尔的早期作品深受贝克特式荒诞戏剧的影响，具有先锋实验性质。卡尔的作品关注男女关系和爱情等主题，如1994年的《梅》（*The Mai*）和接下来的两部戏剧《鲍西亚》（*Portia Coughlan*，1996）、《猫原边……》（*By the Bog of Cats...*，1999）集中刻画了一系列悲剧的女性人物。这三部作品在主题和风格上具有连贯性，被称为“90年代三部曲”，成为卡尔的代表作品。进入新千年，卡尔对戏剧不断探索，不再拘泥于女性主题和以爱尔兰中部为背景的现实风格。《拉夫尔山上》（*On Raftery's Hill*，2000）和《爱丽尔》（*Ariel*，2002）以男性人物为中心，关注现实，内容涉及暴力、腐败、政治、宗教等众多方面。《女人和稻草人》（*Woman and Scarecrow*，2006）和《卡迪亚之梦》（*The Cordelia Dream*，2008）重新开启了实验性探索，以荒诞形式探索女性的存在和价值。

作为成长于后现代主义背景下的女性作家，卡尔用独树一帜的女性姿态、反叛精神和质疑态度，打破了爱尔兰剧坛男性中心和民族叙事的统治局面，为自己确立了毋庸置疑的地位。她关注女性经验。她笔下的女性角色具有鲜明的自我意识，在充满敌意的环境下，以悲壮的反抗姿态发出振聋发聩的声音，同传统戏剧中温顺柔弱、逆来顺受的女性形象形成鲜明对比。卡尔在戏剧中融入了大量的地方元素，包括爱尔兰中部背景和方言，使戏剧呈现出自然粗放的风格，与充满激情的人物相互映衬。卡尔认为理性扼杀了戏剧热情，因此她在承袭爱尔兰讲故事的传统和鬼神文化的基础上，旁征博引，在戏剧中自由插入古希腊戏剧、地方传说、文学文化典故，与戏剧文本形成互文线索，打破时空界限，大大拓展了戏剧空间，呈现出神秘浮动的戏剧效果。通过内容上的无所禁忌和形式上的不拘一格，卡尔用鲜明的个人姿态高调地走入爱尔兰剧坛的聚光灯下，成为当代最重要的爱尔兰女性剧作家。

二、剧情简介

《猫原边……》以爱尔兰少数群落——无地游民（landless travellers）为表现对象，讲述了一位名为“海斯特·斯维恩”（Hester Swan）的女性的悲剧命运。海斯特七岁时被母亲遗弃，在之后的30多年里，她一直在流浪汉群居的沼泽原边苦苦期待母亲的归来。然而，40岁的海斯特始终没有等到她的母亲。相反，海斯特等来的是情人迦太基负心抛弃、另娶有钱农场主的女儿为妻的残酷现实。在沼泽原上，海斯特与迦太基一起生活了14年，并共同育有一个女儿小乔西。在绝望之际，海斯特杀死了她和迦太基的孩子小乔西，她不愿让7岁的孩子重蹈她的覆辙。之后海斯特自杀身亡，全剧终结。

在形式上，剧作家有意将希腊神话之美狄亚的悲剧与海斯特的现实悲剧并行，将海斯特的情人迦太基与古老神话中的同名男主人公相呼应，使具有现代悲剧形象的海斯特在历史对比中向现代的女性命运发问。卡尔利用戏剧的互文循环和鬼迷等超现实哥特效果的营造以及颠覆性的母亲形象共同勾勒出一个不同以往的爱尔兰“黑色田园”，赋予该剧鲜明的后现代特征。

三、名篇选读

By the Bog of Cats...

ACT I　Scene IV

Josie and Mrs. Kilbride enter and sit at the garden table as the Catwoman and Hester exit. Josie is dressed: Wellingtons, trousers, jumper on insider out. They're playing snap[1]*. Mrs. Kilbride plays ruthlessly, lovers to win. Josie looks on in dismay.*

MRS. KILBRIDE: Snap-snap![1] Snap! (*stacking the cards*) How many games is that I'm after winnin' ya?

JOSIE: Five.

MRS. KILBRIDE: And how many did you win?

JOSIE: Ya know right well I won ne'er a game.

MRS. KILBRIDE: And do ya know why ya won ne'er a game, Josie? Because you're thick, that's the why.

JOSIE: I always win when I play me mam.

MRS. KILBRIDE: That's only because your mam is thicker than you. Thick and stubborn and dangerous wrongheaded and backwards to top it all. Are you goin' to start cryin' now, ya little pussy babby; don't you dare cry; ya need to toughen up, child; what age are ya now? I says what age are ya?

JOSIE: Seven.

MRS. KILBRIDE: Seven auld years. When I was seven I was cookin' dinners for a houseful of men. I was thinnin' turnips twelve hour a day. I was birthin' calves, sowin' corn, stookin' hay, ladin' a bull be his nose, and you can't even win a game of snap. Sit up straight or ya'll grow up a hunchback. Would ya like that, would ya, to grow up a hunchback? Ya'd be like an auld[2] camel and everyone'd say, as ya loped by, 'There goes Josie Kilbride the hunchback,' would ya like that, would ya? Answer me.

JOSIE: Ya know right well I wouldn't, granny.

MRS. KILBRIDE: What did I tell ya about callin' me grand-mother?

JOSIE: (*defiantly*) Granny.

MRS. KILBRIDE: (*leans over the table viciously*) Grandmother! Say it!

JOSIE: (*giving in*) Grandmother.

MRS. KILBRIDE: And you're lucky I ever let ya call me that. Ya want another game?

JOSIE: Only if ya don't cheat.

MRS. KILBRIDE: When did I cheat?

JOSIE: I seen ya, loads of times.

MRS. KILBIRDE: A bad loser's all you are, Josie, and there's nothin' meaner than a bad loser. I never cheat. Never. D'ya hear me, do ya? Look me in the eye when I'm talkin' to ya, ya little bastard. D'ya want another game?

JOSIE:	No thanks, Grandmother.
MRS. KILBRIDE:	And why don't ya? Because ya know I'll win, isn't that it? Ya little coward ya, I'll break your spirit yet and then glue ya back the way I want ya. I bet ya can't even spell your name.
JOSIE:	And I bet ya I can.
MRS. KILBIRDE:	G'wan then, spell it.
JOSIE:	(*spells*) J-o-s-i-e K-i-l-b-r-i-d-e.
MRS. KILBRIDE:	Wrong! Wrong! Wrong!
JOSIE:	Well, that's the way Teacher taught me.
MRS. KILBRIDE:	Are you back-answerin' me?
JOSIE:	No, Grandmother.
MRS. KILBRIDE:	Ya got some of it right. Ya got the 'Josie' part right, but ya got the 'Kilbride' part wrong, because you're not a Kilbride. You're a Swane. Can ya spell Swane? Of course ya can't. You're Hester Swane's little bastard. You're not a Kilbride and never will be.
JOSIE:	I'm tellin' Daddy what you said.
MRS. KILBRIDE:	Tell him! Ya won't be tellin' him anythin' I haven't told him meself. He's an eegit, your daddy. I warned him about that wan, Hester Swane, that she'd get her claws in, and she did, the tinker[3]. That's what yees are, tinkers. And your poor daddy, all he's had to put up with. Well, at last that's all changin's now. Why don't yees head off in that auld caravan, back to wherever yees came from, and give your poor daddy back to me where he frightfully belongs? And you've your jumper on backwards.
JOSIE:	It's not backwards, it's inside out.
MRS. KILBRIDE:	Don't you cheek me-and tell me this, Josie Swane; how much has your mam in the bank?
JOSIE:	I don't know.
MRS. KILBRIDE:	I'll tell ya how much, a great big goose egg. Useless, that's what she is, livin' off of handouts from my son that she flitters away on whiskey and cigars, the Jezebel witch[4]. (*smugly*) Guess how much I've saved, Josie, g'wan, guess, guess.

JOSIE: I wish if me mam'd came soon.

MRS. KILBRIDE: (*hysterical*) Ten pound! A'ya mad, child? A'ya mad! Ten pound! (*whispers avariciously*) Three thousand pound. All mine. I saved it. I didn't frig it away on crame buns and blouses. No. I saved it. A thousand for me funeral, a thousand for the Little Sisters of the Poor[5] and a thousand for your daddy. I'm lavin' you nothin' because your mother would get hould of it. And d'ya think would I get any thanks for sabin' all the money? Oh no, none in the world. Would it ever occur to anywan to say, 'Well done, Mrs. Kilbride, well done, Elsie,' not wance did your daddy ever say, 'Well done, Mother,' no, too busy fornicatin' with Hester Swane, too busy bringin' little bastards like yourself into the world.

JOSIE: Can I go and play now?

MRS. KILBRIDE: Here, I brung ya sweets, g'wan ate them, ate them all; there's a great child; ya need some sugar, some sweetie pie sweetness in your life. C'mere and give your auld grandmother a kiss.

(*Josie does.*)

Sure it's not your fault ya were born a little girl bastard. D'ya want another game of snap? I'll let ya win.

JOSIE: No.

MRS. KILBRIDE: Don't you worry, child; we'll get ya off of her yet. Me your daddy has plans. We'll batter ya into the semblance of legitimacy yet, soon as we get ya off—

(*enter Carthage*)

CARTHAGE: I don't know how many times I tould ya to lave the child alone. You've her poisoned with your bile and rage.

MRS. KILBRIDE: I'm sayin' nothin' that isn't true. Can't I play a game of snap with me own granddaughter?

CATHAGE: Ya know I don't want ya around here at the minute. G'wan home, Mother. G'wan!

MRS. KILBRIDE: And do what? Talk to the range? Growl at God?

CARTHAGE: Do whatever ya like, only lave Josie alone, pick on somewan your

	own size. (*He turns Josie's jumper the right way around.*) You'll have to learn to dress yourself.
MRS. KILBRIDE:	Ah now, Carthage, don't be annoyed with me. I only came up to say good-bye to her, found her in her pyjamas out here playin' in the snow. Why isn't her mother mindin' her?
CARTHAGE:	Don't start in on that again.
MRS. KILBRIDE:	I never left you on your own.
CARTHAGE:	Ya should have.
MRS. KILBRIDE:	And ya never called in to see the new dress I got for today and ya promised ya would.
	(*Carthage glares at her.*)
	Alright, I'm goin', I'm goin'. Just don't think now ya've got Caroline Cassidy ya can do away with me, the same as you're doin' away with Hester Swane. I'm your mother and I won't be goin' away. Ever. (*exits*)
CARTHAGE:	Where's your man?
JOSIE:	Isn't she always on the bog[6]? Can I go to your weddin'?
CARTHAGE:	What does your mother say?
JOSIE:	She says there'll be no weddin' and to stop annoyin' her.
CARTHAGE:	We'll see, Josie; we'll see.
JOSIE:	I'll wear me Communion[7] dress. Remember me Communion, Daddy?
CARTHAGE:	I do.
JOSIE:	Wasn't it just a brilliant day?
CARTHAGE:	It was, sweetheart, it was. Come on, we go check the calves.
	(*and exit the pair*)
	(*Exit Caroline. Hester stands there alone, takes a drink, goes into the caravan, comes out with a knife. She tests it for sharpness, teases it across her throat, shivers.*) Come on, ya done it aisy enough to another, now it's your own turn.
	(*Bares her throat, ready to do it. Enter Josie running, stops, sees*

Hester with the knife poised.)

JOSIE: Mam—what's that ya've got there?

HESTER: (*stops*) Just an auld fishin' knife, Josie, I've had this years.

JOSIE: And what are ya doin' with it?

HESTER: Nothin', Josie, nothin'.

JOSIE: I came to say good-bye; we'll be goin' soon. (*kisses Hester*)

HESTER: Good-bye, sweetheart—Josie, ya won't see me again now.

JOSIE: I will so. I'm only goin' on a honeymoon.

HESTER: No, Josie, ya won't see me again because I'm goin' away too.

JOSIE: Where?

HESTER: Somewhere ya can never return from.

JOSIE: And where's that?

HESTER: Never mind. I only wanted to tell ya good-bye, that's all.

JOSIE: Well, can I go with ya?

HESTER: Well, ya can't, because wance ya go there ya can never come back.

JOSIE: I wouldn't want to if you're not here, Mam.

HESTER: You're just bein' contrary now. Don't ya want to be with your daddy and grow up big and lovely and full of advantages I have not the power to give ya?

JOSIE: Mam, I'd be watchin' for ya all the time 'long the Bog of Cats. I'd be hopin' and waitin' and prayin' for ya to return.

HESTER: Don't be sayin' them things to me now.

JOSIE: Just take me with ya, Mam. (*puts her arms around Hester*)

HESTER: (*pushing her away*) No, ya don't understand. Go away; get away from me; g'wan now; run away from me quickly now.

JOSIE: (*frantic*) No, Mam. Please!

HESTER: Alright, alright! Shhh! (*picks her up*) It's alright. I'll take ya with me. I won't have ya as I was, waitin' a lifetime for somewan to return[8], because they don't, Josie, they don't. It's alright. Close your eyes.

(*Josie closes her eyes.*) **Are they closed tight?**

JOSIE: Yeah.

(*Hester cuts Josie's throat in one savage movement.*)

(*softly*) **Mam—Mam—**(*And Josie dies in Hester's arms.*)

HESTER: (*whispers*) It's because ya wanted to come, Josie.

Begins to wail, a terrible animal wail. Enter the Catwoman.

CATWOMAN: Hester, what is it? What is it?

HESTER: Oh, Catwoman, I knew somethin' terrible'd happen, I never thought it'd be this. (*continues this terrible sound, barely recognizable as something human*)

CATWOMAN: What have ya done, Hester? Have ya harmed yourself?

HESTER: No, not meself and yes meself.

CATWOMAN: (*comes over, feels around Hester, feels Josie*) Not Josie, Hester? Not Josie? Lord on high, Hester, not the child. I thought yourself, maybe, or Carthage, but never the child. (*runs to the edge of the stage shouting*) Help, somewan, help! Hester Swane's after butcherin' the child! Help!

(*Hester walks around demented with Josie. Enter Carthage running.*)

CARTHAGE: What is it, Catwoman? Hester? What's wrong with Josie? There's blood all over her.

HESTER: (*brandishing knife*) Lave off, you. Lave off. I warned ya and I tould ya. Would ya listen. What've I done. What've I done?

(*enter Monica*)

CARTHAGE: Give her to me!

MONICA: Sweet Jesus, Hester—

CARTHAGE: Give her to me! You've killed her; she's killed her.

HESTER: Yees all thought I was just goin' to walk away and lave her at yeer mercy. I almost did. But she's mine and I wouldn't have her waste her life dreamin' about me and yees thwartin' her with black stories against me.

CARTHAGE: You're a savage!

(*Enter the Ghost Fancier*[9]. *Hester sees him; the others don't. He picks up the fishing knife.*)

HETSER: You're late; ya came too late.

CARTHAGE: What's she sayin'? What? Give her to me, come on now. (*takes Josie off Hester*)

HESTER: Ya won't forget me now, Carthage, and when all of this is over or half remembered and you think you've almost forgotten me again, take a walk along the Bog of Cats and wait for a purlin' wind through your hair or a soft breath be your ear or a rustle behind ya. That'll be me and Josie ghostin' ya. (*She walks towards the Ghost Fancier.*) Take me away; take me away from here.

GHOST FANCIER: Alright, my lovely.

(*They go into a death dance with the fishing knife, which ends plunged into Hester's heart. She falls to the ground. Exits Ghost Fancier with knife.*)

HESTER: (*whispers as she dies*) Mam—Mam—

(*Monica goes over to her after a while.*)

MONICA: Hester—she's gone—Hester—she's cut her heart out—it's lyin' there on top of her chest like some dark feathered bird[10].

(*Music. Lights*)

END OF PLAY

注释

1. **snap:** 爱尔兰的一种扑克牌游戏，也叫“捉对儿”。
2. **auld:** “old”的古英语。爱尔兰中部地区的方言中仍保留了一些古英语单词。
3. **tinker:** 补锅匠，特别指爱尔兰的流浪者，他们常靠补锅为生。这是对他们的蔑称。
4. **Jezebel witch:** 《圣经》中《列王记上》里的人物。Jezebel字面的意思是“贞洁”，但实际上这个人无耻且邪恶。
5. **Little Sisters of the Poor:** 安贫小姐妹会。1839年建立的罗马天主教组织，致力于照顾生活贫困的老人。

6. **bog:** 沼泽，爱尔兰重要地貌。这里积聚着泥煤，覆盖着杜鹃科的植被。这种地貌独特而神秘，常出现在文学作品中，也是本剧的重要背景。
7. **communion:** 圣餐仪式，天主教给孩子的第二次洗礼，8岁左右的孩子去教堂领第一次圣餐举行的仪式。孩子们必须盛装出席。女孩穿婚纱般的礼服，男孩穿西服。天主教在爱尔兰人民的生活中扮演重要角色，因此这个仪式非常隆重。
8. **waitin a lifetime for womewan to return:** 剧中主人公Hester在7岁时被母亲遗弃，她从此在猫原边上盼望母亲回来。
9. **ghost Fancier:** 鬼迷，剧中虚幻的角色。
10. **dark feathered bird:** 黑天鹅。剧中Hester的母亲在她出生那天就将她放进黑天鹅的窝里，声称是因为她们的姓Swan意为“天鹅”，之后她更预言Hester会与黑天鹅在同一天死去，结果预言成真。

四、拓展思考

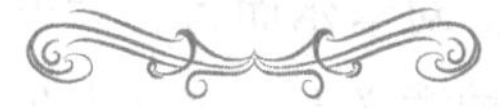

1. What's your understanding of the image 'G'wan'?
2. Please use your words to describe the image of the Grandmother. The image of (Grand) mother in the play sets a sharp contrast with that in Yeats' Cathleen. How do you understand the differences?
3. Why did Hester kill her daughter? Compare it with the old Grecian tale and try to understand the tragic significance of the play.
4. Why is this play entitled as *By The Bog of Cats...*? Try to read the play by Synge and acquire more knowledge about the social status of the minority group in Ireland.

五、延展阅读

作为90年代的新生力量，卡尔并不像男性剧作家们那样喜欢在舞台上戏剧化地直接处理宏大的“社会与文化问题”。卡尔的作品在内容上以女性为视角，关注女性的精神生存状态，其剧中的女性无一不是充满悲伤和泪水的。在表现形式上，卡尔擅长于从古典中汲取创作灵感，运用大量的神话故事、地方传说或文学经典，构筑虚幻和现实的双层空间。她相信超现实力量和他者世界。希腊神话中无法挣脱的宿命构成了卡尔剧作的核心。她的作品中有哥特式风格的当代再现，如鬼迷、巫女，并以虚幻的形式存在。

同时，这一双层的构架辅之以独白式的回忆叙述，努力探讨梦境和心理的无意识层面，逐步摆脱现实主义束缚的内心世界。多种记忆构成对同一事物的不同回忆，如本章的《猫原边……》中不同人对于大乔西的记忆描述，形成与海斯特自己对母亲记忆的差异。多种的形象留白留给读者（观众）判断，进而在产生不确定性的同时加深悲剧色彩。

无论是内容还是形式，卡尔的剧作都给读者提供了丰富的爱尔兰文化元素和解读可能，在《猫原边……》中就可以窥视剧作家的宗教态度。从剧中天主教的代表威洛牧师的疯疯癫癫和对天主教的讽刺，以及与异教徒女巫（猫妇）的形象设计中，可以看出怪诞形式下对权威——神圣宗教的颠覆。

在卡尔的剧作里，宗教、传统、民俗存在于一个个的女性人物塑造中，更准确地说是女性与国家的象征中，这体现了一位当代女性作家对20世纪爱尔兰社会的观察和艺术呈现。正如一位评论家所言："卡尔的成功在于她的作品表现了文化发展中伴随的社会不稳定性——一个仍面临黑暗的世界"。对卡尔而言，"卡尔戏剧的中心是家庭，从这个小世界折射出文化和国家形象。"从某种意义上，包括卡尔在内的新生一代剧作家，都不自觉地集体呈现出爱尔兰的"黑色田园"，打破了以往田园化的爱尔兰乡村形象。

CHAPTER 11

马丁·麦克多纳

Martin McDonagh

《丽南镇的美人》

The Beauty Queen of Leenane

一、剧作家简介

马丁·麦克多纳（Martin McDonagh）是20世纪90年代成长起来的一位爱尔兰剧作家。他和玛丽娜·卡尔被公认为90年代新生力量中最重要的代表人物。他们以典型的后现代风格展现了爱尔兰90年代以来戏剧创作的新貌。

麦克多纳年少成名，被誉为“神童剧作家”（a playwright prodigy）。1996年，他的处子秀《丽南镇的美人》（*The Beauty Queen of Leenane*）上演后即刻轰动。在接下来的两年间，他的另外三部戏剧：《康尼马拉的骷髅》（*A Skull in Connermara*，1997）、《荒漠的西部》（*The Lonesome West*，1997）和《伊尼什曼岛的瘸子》（*The Cripple of Inishmaan*，1996）相继上演，构成了他的“丽南镇三部曲”和“阿兰岛三部曲”的首曲。“27岁就有四部剧同时在伦敦上演，也只有莎士比亚一人而已”，因此麦克多纳被媒体视为“最有希望的剧作家”。

麦克多纳同时又是一位备受争议的剧作家。他夸张荒诞的黑色喜剧和“直面戏剧”（In-Yer-Face Theatre，又译扑面戏剧）的舞台艺术，引发了各个年龄层次观众的热议。他被观众追捧成“绿翡翠岛上的昆丁”（Quentin Tarontino of the Emerald Isle）和“麦克多纳神话”（McDonagh Enigma）的同时，又被痛骂为“流星、大嘴巴剧作家”。他受到的赞誉和非议并存，形成舆论的两极。

麦克多纳是一个具有双重性文化身份的作家。一方面，他出生于伦敦，成长于流行文化蔓延的时代，爱听朋克音乐、爱看电影和肥皂剧。在戏剧创作上，他完全认同英国90年代“直面戏剧”的美学原则；另一方面，因父母是爱尔兰人，麦克多纳在少年时代每年夏天都会随父母回爱尔兰西部度假，这使他对爱尔兰有着特殊的感情，故而他的戏剧多以爱尔兰西部高威为场景，体现出了鲜明的爱尔兰性。麦克多纳在90年代以新锐作家的姿态，更新着人们对爱尔兰人、爱尔兰性、爱尔兰文化、爱尔兰身份的传统认知。

二、剧情简介

《丽南镇的美人》是麦克多纳的首部戏剧，也是他的重要剧作之一。该剧以爱尔兰西部高威郡的小镇——“丽南镇”为背景，描述了一对贫困母女的故事。已到中年的女儿莫兰（Maureen）和她的恋人佩托一心想离开闭塞落后的丽南镇。但莫兰年迈的母亲麦格（Mag）却只想将女儿牢牢地拴在身边，反对女儿莫兰与佩托相爱，并极力阻止莫兰随佩托去美国。尽管母亲成功了，但反抗的莫兰最终将滚烫的热油倒在母亲手上，将母亲杀死。然而，母亲的去世并没有使莫兰获得原来期待的解脱和自由，而彻底成为精神上瘫痪的行尸走肉。剧尾，莫兰坐在母亲生前的摇椅上，想象着母亲的模样，伴随着背景歌曲“旋转的车轮”（The Spinning Wheel）而陷入惆怅。场景对于人物命运的暗示有着极大的讽刺效果。该剧在骇人、残酷、荒诞的表象下，突出了剧中人物心理上的无力和失落感。

此外，剧中的人物塑造也极具象征意义。母亲麦格是“一个70开外、微胖的女人”，这很容易让观众联想到爱尔兰立国迄今的历史，并将麦格与爱尔兰戏剧舞台上经典的老妇人与民族象征形象形成逻辑关联。母亲总是躺在摇椅上，无力站起。晃动中的摇椅，总处于一种变动不居的状态，具有象征意味。本篇节选自该剧的第七场、第八场和第九场。

三、名篇选读

The Beauty Queen of Leenane

Scene VII

*Night. **Mag** is in her rocking-chair, **Maureen** at the table, reading. The radio is on low, tuned to a request show. The reception is quite poor, wavering and crackling with static. Pause before **Mag** speaks.*

MAG: A poor reception.[1]

MAUREEN: Can I help it if it's a poor reception?

MAG: (*pause*) Crackly. (*pause*) We can hardly hear the tunes. (*pause*) We can hardly hear what are the dedications or from what part of the country.

MAUREEN: I can hear well enough.

MAG: Can ya?

MAUREEN: (*pause*) Maybe it's deaf it is you're going.

MAG: It's not deaf I'm going. Not nearly deaf.

MAUREEN: It's a home[2] for deaf people. I'll have to be putting you in soon, (*pause*) and it isn't cod in butter sauce you'll be getting in there. No. Not by a long chalk. Oul beans on toast or something is all you'll be getting in there. If you're lucky. And then if you don't eat it, they'll give you a good kick, or maybe a punch.

MAG: (*pause*) I'd die before I'd let myself be put in a home.

MAUREEN: Hopefully, aye.

MAG: (*pause*) That was a nice bit of cod in butter sauce, Maureen.

MAG: Tasty.

MAUREEN: All I do is boil it in the bag and snip it with a scissor. I hardly need your compliments.

MAG: (*pause*) Mean to me is all you ever are nowadays.

MAUREEN: If I am or if I'm not. (*pause*) I didn't I buy you a packet of wine gums last week if I'm so mean?

MAG: (*pause*) All because of Pato Dooley[3] you're mean, I suppose (*pause*) him not inviting you to his oul going-away do tonight.

MAUREEN: Pato Dooley has his own life to lead.

MAG: Only after one thing that man was.

MAUREEN: Maybe he was, now. Or maybe it was me who was only after one thing. We do have equality nowadays. Not like in your day.

MAG: There was nothing wrong in my day.

MAUREEN: Allowed to go on top of a man nowadays, we are.[4] All we have to do is ask. And nice it is on top of a man, too.

MAG: Is it nice now, Maureen?

MAUREEN: (*bemused that Mag isn't offended*) It is.

MAG: It does sound nice. Ah, good enough for yourself, now.

(*Maureen still bemused, gets some shortbread fingers*[5] *from the kitchen and eats a couple.*)

MAG: And not worried about having been put in the family way, are you?

MAUREEN: I'm not. We are careful.

MAG: Was ye careful?

MAUREEN: Aye. We was nice and careful, aye. Oh aye. Lovely and careful, I'll bet ye were.

MAUREEN: (*pause*) You haven't been sniffing the paraffin lamps again?

MAG: (*pause*) It's always the paraffin lamp business you do throw at me.

MAUREEN: It's a funny oul mood you're in so.

MAG: Is it a funny oul mood? No. Just a normal mood, now.

MAUREEN: It's a funny one. (*pause*) Aye, a great oul time me and Pato did have. I can see now what all the fuss did he about, but ah, there has to be more to a man than just being good in bed. Things in common too you do have to have, y'know, like what books do you be reading, or what are your politics and the like. So I did have to tell him it was no-go, no matter how good in bed he was.

MAG: When was this you did tell him?

MAUREEN: A while ago it was I did tell him. Back...

MAG: (*interrupting*) And I suppose he was upset at that.

MAUREEN: He *was* upset at that but I assured him it was for the best and he did seem to accept it then.

MAG: I'll bet he accepted it.

MAUREEN: (*pause*) But that's why Ii thought it would be unfair of me to go over to his do and wish him goodbye. I thought it would be awkward for him.

MAG: It would be awkward for him, aye, I suppose. Oh aye. (*pause*) So all it was was ye didn't have enough things in common was all that parted ye?

MAUREEN: Is all it was. And parted on amicable terms, and with no grudges on either side. (*pause*) No. No grudges at all. I did get what I did want out of Pato Dooley that night, and that was good enough for him, and that was good enough for me.

MAG: Oh aye, now. I'm sure. It was good enough for the both of ye. Oh aye.

(*Mag smiles and nods.*)

MAUREEN: (*laughing*) It's crazy oul mood you're in for yourself tonight! Pleased that tonight it is Pato's leaving and won't be coming pawing me again is what it is, I bet.

MAG: Maybe that's what it is. I am glad Pato's leaving.

MAUREEN: (*smiling*) An interfering oul biddy is all you are. (*pause*) Do you want a shortbread finger?

MAG: I do want a shortbread finger.

MAUREEN: Please.

MAG: Please.

(*Maureen gives Mag a shortbread finger, after waving it phallically in the air a moment.*)

MAUREEN: Remind me of something, shortbread fingers do.

MAG: I suppose they do, now.

MAUREEN: I suppose it's so long since you've seen what they remind me of, you do forget what they look like.

MAG: I suppose I do. And I suppose you're the expect.

MAUREEN: I am the expert.

MAG: Oh aye.

MAUREEN: I'm the king of the experts.

MAG: I suppose you are, now. Oh, I'm sure. I suppose you're the king of the experts.

MAUREEN: (*pause, suspicious*) Why wouldn't you be sure?

MAG: With your Pato Dooley and your throwing it all in me face like and oul peahen, eh? When... (*Mag catches herself before revealing any more.*)

MAUREEN: (*pause, smiling*) When what?

MAG: Not another word on the subject am I saying. I do have no comment, as they say. This is a nice shortbread finger.

MAUREEN: (*with an edge*) When what, now?

MAG: (*getting sacred*) When nothing, Maureen.

MAUREEN: (*forcefully*) No, when what, now? (*pause*) Have you been speaking to somebody?

MAG: Who would I be speaking to, Maureen?

MAUREEN: (*trying to work it out*) You've been speaking to somebody. You've...

MAG: Nobody have I been speaking to, Maureen. You know well I don't be speaking to anybody. And, sure, who would Pato be telling about that...?

(*MAG suddenly realises what she said. Maureen stares at her in dumb shock and hate, then walks to the kitchen, dazed, puts a chip-pan on the stove, turns it on high and pours a half-bottle of cooking oil into it, takes down the rubber gloves that are hanging the back wall and puts them on. Mag puts her hands on the arms of the rocking-chair to drag herself up, but Maureen shoves a foot against her stomach and groin, ushering her back. Mag leans back into the chair, frightened, staring at Maureen, who sits at the table, waiting for the oil to boil. She speaks quietly, staring straight ahead.*)

MAUREEN: How do you know?

MAG: Nothing do I know, Maureen.

MAUREEN: Uh-huh?

MAG: (*pause*) Or was it Ray[6] did mention something? Aye, I think it was Ray...

MAUREEN: Nothing to Ray would Pato've said about that subject.

MAG: (*tearfully*) Just to stop you bragging like an oul peahen, was I saying, Maureen. Sure what does an oul woman like me know? Just guessing, I was.

MAUREEN: You know sure enough, and guessing me arse, and not on me face was it written. For the second time and for the last time I'll be asking, now. How do you know?

MAG: On your face it was written, Maureen. Sure that's the only way I knew. You still do have the look of a virgin about you you always have had.

(*without malice*) You always will.

(*Pause. The oil has started boiling. Maureen rises, turns the radio up, stares at Mag as she passes her, takes the pan off the boil and turns the gas off, and returns to Mag with it.*)

MAG: (*terrified*) A letter he did send you I read!

(*Maureen slowly and deliberately takes her mother's shrivelled hand, holds it down on the burning range, and starts slowly pouring some of the hot oil over it, as Mag screams in pain and terror.*)

MAUREEN: Where is the letter?

MAG: (*through screams*) I did burn it! I'm sorry, Maureen!

MAUREEN: What did the letter say?

(*Mag is screaming so much that she can't answer. Maureen stops pouring the oil and releases the hand, which mag clutches to herself, doubled-up, still screaming, crying and whimpering.*)

MAUREEN: What did the letter say?

MAG: Said he did have too much to drink, it did! Is why, and not your fault at all.

MAUREEN: And what else did it say?

MAG: He won't be putting me into no home!

MAUREEN: What are you talking about, no home? What else did it say?!

MAG: I can't remember, now, Maureen. I can't...!

(*Maureen grabs Mag's hand, holds it down again and repeats the torture.*)

MAG: No...!

MAUREEN: What else did it say?! Eh?!

MAG: (*through screams*) Asked you to go to America with him, it did!

(*Stunned, Maureen releases Mag's hand and stops pouring the oil. Mag clutches her hand to herself again, whimpering.*)

MAUREEN: What?

MAG: But how could you go with him? You do still have me to look after.

MAUREEN: (*in a happy daze*) He asked me to go to America with him? Pato asked me to go to America with him?

MAG: (*looking up at her*) But what about me, Maureen?

(*A slight pause before Maureen, in a single and almost lazy motion, throws the considerable remainder of the oil into Mag's midriff, some of it splashing up into her face. Mag doubles-up, screaming, falls to the floor, trying to pat the oil off her, and lies there convulsing, screaming and whimpering. Maureen steps out of her way to avoid her fall, still in a daze, barely noticing her.*)

MAUREEN: (*dreamily, to herself*) He asked me to go to America with him...? (*recovering herself*) What time is it? Oh feck, he'll be leaving! I've got to see him. Oh God... What will I wear? Uh... Me black dress[7]! Me little black dress! It'll be a remembrance to him... (*darts off through the hall*)

MAG: (*quietly, sobbing*) Maureen... help me...

(*Maureen returns a moment later, pulling her black dress on.*)

MAUREEN: (*to herself*) How do I look? Ah, I'll have to do. What time is it? Oh God...

MAG: Help me, Maureen...

MAUREEN: (*brushing her hair*) Help you, is it? After what you've done? Help you, she says. No, I won't help you, and I'll tell you another thing. If you've made me miss Pato before he goes, then you'll really be for it, so you will, and no messing this time. Out of me fecking way, now...

(*Maureen steps over Mag, who is still shaking on the floor, and exits through the front door. Pause. Mag is still crawling around slightly. The front door bangs open and Mag looks up at Maureen as she breezes back in.*)

MAG: Me car keys I forgot...

(*MAUREEN grabs her keys from the table, goes to the door, turns back to the table and switches the radio off.*)

(*Maureen exits again, slamming the door. Pause. Sound of her car starting and pulling off. Pause.*)

MAG: (*quietly*) But who'll look after me, so?

(*Mag still shaking, looks down at her scalded hand. Blackout.*)

Scene VIII

Same night. The only light in the room emanates from the orange coals through the grill of the range, just illuminating the dark shapes of Mag, sitting in her rocking-chair, which rocks back and forth of its own volition, her body unmoving, and Maureen, still in her black dress, who idles very slowly around the room, poker in hand.

MAUREEN: To Boston. To Boston I'll be going. Isn't that where them two were from, the Kennedys[8], or was that somewhere else, now? Robert Kennedy I did prefer over Jack Kennedy. He seemed to be nicer to women. Although I haven't read up on it. (*pause*) Boston. It does have a nice ring to it. Better than England it'll be, I'm sure. Although where wouldn't be better than England? [9] No shite I'll be cleaning there, anyways, and no names called, and Pato'll be there to have a say-so anyways if there was to be names called, but I'm sure there won't be. The Yanks do love the Irish. (*pause*) Almost begged me, Pato did. Almost on his hands and knees, he was, near enough crying. At the station I caught him, not five minutes to spare, thanks to you. Thanks to your oul interfering, but too late to be interfering you are now. Oh aye. Be far too late, although you did give it a good go, I'll say that for you. Another five minutes and you'd have had it. Poor you. Poor selfish oul bitch, oul you. (*pause*) Kissed the face off me, he did, when he saw me there. Them blue eyes of his. Them muscles. Them arms wrapping me. "Why did you not answer me letter?" And all for coming over and giving you a good kick he was when I told him, but "Ah no," I said, 'isn't she just a feeble-minded oul feck, not worth dirtying your boots on?' I was defending you there. (*pause*) "You will come to Boston with me so, me love, when you get up the money." "I will, Pato. Be it married or be it living in sin, what do I care? What do I care if tongues'd be wagging? Tongues have wagged about me before, let them wag again. Let them never stop wagging, so long as I'm with you, Pato, What do I care about tongues? So long as it's you and me, and the warmth of us cuddled up, and the skins of us asleep, is all I ever really wanted anyway." (*pause*) "Except we do still have a problem, what to do with your oul mam, there," he said. "Would an oul folks home be too harsh?" "It wouldn't be too harsh but it would be too expensive." "What about your sisters so?" "Me sisters wouldn't have the bitch. Not even a half-day at Christmas to be with her can them two stand. They clear forgot her birthday this year as well as that." "How do you stick her without going off your rocker?" They do say to me. Behind her back, like. (*pause*) "I'll leave it up to yourself so," Pato says. He was on the train be this time; we was kissing out the window, like they do in films.[10] I'll leave it up to yourself so, whatever you decide. If it takes a month, let it take a month. And if it's finally you decide you can't bear to be parted from her and have to stay behind, well, I can't say I would like it, but I'd understand. But if even a year it has to take for you to decide, it is a year I will be waiting, and won't be minding the wait." "It won't be a year it is you'll be waiting, Pato", I called out then; the train was pulling away. "It won't be a year nor yet nearly a year. It won't be a week!"

The rocking-chair has stopped its motions. Mag starts to slowly lean forward at the waist until she finally topples over and falls heavily to the floor, dead. A red chunk of skull hangs from a string of skin at the side of her head. Maureen looks down at her, somewhat bored, taps her on the side with he toe of her shoe, then steps onto her back and stands there in thoughtful contemplation.

'Twas over the stile she did trip. Aye. And down the hill she did fall. Aye. (pause) Aye.

Pause. Blackout.

Scene IX

A rainy afternoon. Front door opens and Maureen enters in funeral attire, takes her jacket off and idles around quietly, her mind elsewhere. She lights a fire in the range, turns the radio on low and sits down in the rocking-chair. After a moment she half-laughs, takes down the boxes of Complan[11] and porridge from the kitchen shelf, goes back to the range and empties the contents of both on the fire. She exits into the hall and returns a moment later with an old suitcase which she lays on the table, brushing off a thick layer of dust. She opens it, considers for a second what she needs to pack, hen returns to the hall. There is a knock at the door. Maureen returns, thinks a moment, takes the suitcase off the table and places it to one side, fixes her hair a little, then answers the door.

MAUREEN: Oh hello there, Ray.

RAY: (*off*) Hello there, Mrs...

MAUREEN: Come in ahead for yourself.

RAY: I did see you coming ahead up the road.

(*Ray enters, closing the door*. **Maureen** *idles to the kitchen and makes herself some tea.*)

RAY: I didn't think so early you would be back. Did you not want to go on to the reception or the what you call they're having at Rory's[12] so?

MAUREEN: No. I do have better things to do with me time.

RAY: Aye, aye. Have your sisters gone on to it?

MAUREEN: They have, aye.

RAY: Of course. Coming back here after, will they be?

MAUREEN: Going straight home, I think they said they'd be.

RAY: Oh aye. Sure, it's a long oul drive for them. Or fairly long. (*pause*) It did all go off okay, then?

MAUREEN: It did.

RAY: Despite the rain.

MAUREEN: Despite the rain.

RAY: A poor oul day for a funeral.

MAUREEN: It was. When it could've been last month we buried her, and she could've got the last of the sun, if it wasn't for the hundred bastarding inquests, proved nothing.

RAY: You'll be glad that's all over and done with now, anyways.

MAUREEN: Very glad.

RAY: I suppose they do only have their jobs to do. (*pause*) Although no fan am I of the bastarding polis. Me two wee toes they went and broke on me for no reason, me arsehole drunk and disorderly.

MAUREEN: The polis broke your toes, did they?

RAY: They did.

MAUREEN: Some bull.

RAY: Some bull, is it? No. Asking about your mam's funeral, I was.

MAUREEN: That's what I'm saying.

RAY: (*pause*) Was there a big turn-out at it?

MAUREEN: Me sisters and one of their husbands and nobody else but Maryjohnny Rafferty and oul Father Walsh-Welsh -saying the thing.

RAY: Father Welsh punched Mairtin Hanlon in the head once, and for no reason.[13] (*pause*) Are you not watching telly for yourself, no?

MAUREEN: I'm not. It's only Australian oul shite[14] they do ever show on that thing.

RAY: (*slightly bemused*) Sure, that's why I do like it. Who wants to see Ireland on telly?

MAUREEN: I do.

RAY: All you have to do is look out your window to see Ireland. And it's soon bored you'd be. 'There goes a calf.' (*pause*) I be bored anyway. I be continually bored. (*pause*) London I'm thinking of going to. Aye. Thinking of it, anyways. To work, y'know. One of these days. Or else Manchester. They have a lot more drugs in Manchester. Supposedly, anyways.

MAUREEN: Don't be getting messed up in drugs, now, Ray, for yourself. Drugs are terrible dangerous.

RAY: Terrible dangerous, are they? Drugs, now?

MAUREEN: You know full well they are.

RAY: Maybe they are; maybe they are. But there are plenty of other things just as dangerous, would kill you just as easy. Maybe even easier.

MAUREEN: (*wary*) Things like what, now?

RAY: (*pause, shrugging*) This bastarding town for one.

MAUREEN: (*pause, sadly*) Is true enough.

RAY: Just that it takes seventy years. Well, it won't take me seventy years. I'll tell you that. No way, boy. (*pause*) How old was your mother, now, when she passed?

MAUREEN: Seventy, aye. Bang on.

RAY: She had a good innings, anyway. (*pause*) Or an innings, anyway. (*sniffs the air*) What's this you've been burning?

MAUREEN: Porridge and Complan I've been burning.

RAY: For why?

MAUREEN: Because I don't eat porridge or Complan. The remainders of me mother's, they were. I was having a good clear-out.

RAY: Only a waste that was.

MAUREEN: Do I need your say-so so?

RAY: I'd've been glad to take them off your hands, I'm saying.

MAUREEN: (*quietly*) I don't need your say-so.

RAY: The porridge, anyway. I do like a bit of porridge. I'd've left the Complan. I don't drink complan. Never had no call to.

MAUREEN: There's some Kimberleys[15] left in the packet I was about to burn too; you can have, if it's such a big thing.

RAY: I will have them Kimberleys. I do love Kimberleys.

MAUREEN: I bet you do.

(*Ray eats a couple of Kimberleys.*)

RAY: Are they a bit stale, now? (*chews*) It does be hard to tell with Kimberleys. (*pause*) I think kimberleys are me favourite biscuits out of any biscuits. Them or Jaffa Cakes. (*pause*) Or Wagon Wheels[16]. (*pause*) Or would you classify Wagon Wheels as biscuits at all now. Aren't they more of a kind of a bar..?

MAUREEN: (*interrupting*) I've things to do now. Ray. Was it some reason you has to come over or was it just to discuss Wagon Wheels?

RAY: Oh aye, now. No, I did have a letter from Pato the other day and he did ask me to come up.

(*Maureen sits in the rocking-chair and listens with keen interest.*)

MAUREEN: He did? What did he have to say?

RAY: He said sorry to hear about your mother and all, and his condolences he sent.

MAUREEN: Aye, aye, aye, and anything else, now?

RAY: That was the main gist of it, the message he said to pass onto you.

MAUREEN: It had no times or details, now?

RAY: Times or details? No...

MAUREEN: I suppose...

RAY: Eh?

MAUREEN: Eh?

RAY: Eh? Oh, also he said he was sorry he didn't get to see you the night he left, there; he would've likes to've said goodbye. But if that was the way you wanted it, so be it. Although rude, too, I thought that was.

MAUREEN: (*standing, confused*) I did see him the night he left. At the station, there.

RAY: What station? Be taxicab Pato left. What are you thinking of?

MAUREEN: (*sitting*) I don't know now.

RAY: Be taxicab Pato left, and sad that he never got your goodbye, although why he wanted your goodbye I don't know. (*pause*) I'll tell you this, Maureen, not being harsh, but your house does smell an awful lot nicer now that your mother's dead. I'll say it does, now.

MAUREEN: Well, isn't that the best? With me thinking I did see him the night he left, there. The train that pulled away.

(*He looks at her as if she's mad.*)

RAY: Aye, aye. (*Mumbled, sarcastic.*) Have a rest for yourself. (*pause*) Oh, do you know a lass called,em... Dolores Hooley, or Healey, now? She was over with the Yanks when they was over.

MAUREEN: I know the name, aye.

RAY: She was at me uncle's do they has there, dancing with me brother early on. You remember?

MAUREEN: Dancing with him, was it? Throwing herself at him would be nearer the mark. Like a cheap oul whore.

RAY: I don't know about that, now.

MAUREEN: Something about this Dolores Hooley or whoever she fecking is.

RAY: Oh aye. Herself and Pato did get engaged a week ago, now, he wrote and told me.

MAUREEN: (*shocked*) Engaged to do what?

RAY: Engaged to get married. What do you usually get engaged for? 'Engaged to do what?' Engaged to eat a bun!

(*Maureen is dumbstruck.*)

RAY: A bit young for him, I think, but good luck to him. A whirlwind oul what you call. July next year, they're thinking of having it, but I'll have to write and tell him to move it either forward or back, else it'll coincide with the European championships. I wonder if they'll have the European championships on telly over there at all? Probably not, now, the Yankee bastards. They don't care about football at all. Ah well. (*pause*) It won't be much of a change for her anyways, from Hooley to Dooley. Only one letter. The 'h'. That'll be a good thing. (*pause*) Unless it's Healey that she is. I can't remember. (*pause*) If it's Healey, it'll be three letters. The 'h', the 'e' and 'a'. (*pause*) Would you want me to be passing any message on, now, when I'm writing, Mrs? I'm writing tomorrow.

MAUREEN: I get... I do get confused. Dolores Hooley...?

RAY: (*pause, irritated*) Would you want me to be passing on any message, now, I'm saying?

MAUREEN: (*pause*) Dolores Hooley...?

RAY: (*sighing*) Fecking... The loons you do get in this house! Only repeating!

MAUREEN: Who's a loon?

RAY: Who's a loon, she says!

(*Ray scoffs and turns away, looking out the window. Maureen quietly picks up the poker from beside the range and, holding it low at her side, slowly approaches him from behind.*)

MAUREEN: (*angrily*) Who's a loon?

(*suddenly sees something hidden behind a couple of boxes on the inner window ledge.*)

RAY: (*angrily*) Well, isn't that fecking just the fecking best yet...!

(*Ray picks up a faded tennis ball with a string out of it from the ledge and spins around to confront Maureen with it, so angry that he doesn't even notice the poker. Maureen stops in her tracks.*)

Sitting on the fecking shelf all these fecking years you've has it, and what good did it do ya? A tenner that swingball set did cost me poor ma and da and in 1979 that was, when a tenner was a lot of money. The best fecking present I did ever get and only two oul months' play out of it I got before you went and confiscated it on me. What right did you have? What right at all? No right. And just left it sitting there then to fade to fecking skitter. I wouldn't minded if you'd got some use out of it, if you'd taken the string out and played pat-ball or something agin a wall, but no. Just out of pure spite is the only reason you kept it, and right under me fecking noise. And then you go wondering who's a fecking loon, lady. You're a fecking loon!

(*Maureen lets the poker fall to the floor with a clatter and sits in the rocking-chair, dazed.*)

MAUREEN: I don't know why I did keep your swingball on you, Raymond. I can't remember at all, now. I think me head was in a funny oul way in them days.

RAY: 'In them days,' she says, as she pegs a good poker on the floor and talks about trains.

(*Ray picks the poker up and puts it in its place.*)

That's a good poker, that is. Don't be banging it against anything hard like that, now.

MAUREEN: I won't.

RAY: That's an awful good poker. (*pause*) To show there's no hard feelings over me swingball, will you sent me that poker, Mrs.? A fiver I'll give you.

MAUREEN: Ah, I don't want to be selling me poker now, Ray.

RAY: G'wan. Six!

MAUREEN: No. It does have sentimental value to me.

RAY: I don't forgive you, so!

MAUREEN: Ah, don't be like that, now, Ray...

RAY: No, I don't forgive you at all.

(*Ray goes to the front door and opens it.*)

MAUREEN: Ray! Are you writing to your brother, so?

RAY: (*sighing*) I am. Why?

MAUREEN: Will you be passing a message on from me?

RAY: (*sighs*) Messages, messages, messages, messages! What's the message, so? And make it a short one.

MAUREEN: Just say...

(*Maureen thinks about it a while.*)

RAY: This week, if you can!

MAUREEN: Just say... Just say, 'the beauty queen of Leenane[17] says hello.' That's all.

RAY: "The beauty queen of Leenance says hello."

MAUREEN: Aye. No!

(*Ray sighs again.*)

MAUREEN: Goodbye. Goodbye. 'The beauty queen of Leenane says goodbye.'

RAY: 'The beauty queen of Leenane says goodbye.' Whatever the feck that means, I'll pass it on. 'The beauty queen of Leenane says goodbye', although after this fecking swingball business, I don't see why the feck I should. Goodbye to you so, Mrs...

MAUREEN: Will you turn the radio up a bitten too, before you go, there, Pato, now? Ray, I mean...

RAY: (*exasperated*) Feck...

(*Ray turns the radio up.*)

RAY: The exact fecking image of your mother you are, sitting there pegging orders and forgetting me name! Goodbye!

MAUREEN: And pull the door after you...

RAY: (*shouting angrily*) I was going to pull the fecking door after me!

(*Ray slams the door behind him as he exits. Pause. Maureen starts rocking slightly in the chair, listening to the song by the Chieftains on the radio. The announcer's quiet, soothing voice is then heard.*)

Announcer: A lovely tune from The Chieftains there. This next one, now, goes out from Annette and Margo Folan to their mother Maggie, all the way out in the mountains of Leenane, a lovely part of the world there, on the occasion of her seventy-first birthday last month now. Well, we hope you has a happy one, Maggie, and we hope there'll be a good many more of them to come on top of it. I'm sure there will. This one's for you, now.

(*"The spinning wheel" by Delia Murphy is played. Maureen gently rocks in the chair until about the middle of the fourth verse, when she quietly gets up, picks up the dusty suitcase, caresses it slightly, moves slowly to the hall door and looks back at the empty rocking-chair a while. It is still rocking gently. Slight pause, then Maureen exits into the hall, closing its door behind her as she goes. We listen to the song on the radio to the end, as the chair gradually stops rocking and the lights, very slowly, fade to black.*)

注释

1. **a poor reception:** 信号差。Mag在收音机旁等待收听另外两个女儿为她生日点的歌。
2. **home:** 养老院。
3. **Pato Dooley:** 剧中人物，曾与Maureen约会过的一个当地男子。
4. 本句语序不符合英语标准规范。这是爱尔兰语的一种表达方式，由此彰显作者有别于英国人的文化身份，下文中有多处类似的句子。
5. **shortbread fingers:** 奶油酥棍，由白糖、面粉和黄油制成，和手指差不多大小。
6. **Ray:** Pato的弟弟。
7. **black dress:** Maureen和Pato第一次约会时穿的黑裙子。
8. **Kennedys:** 肯尼迪兄弟，美国显赫的政治人物，是爱尔兰逃荒到美国的移民后裔。
9. 这句话表达了Mareen对英国的憎恨。历史上爱尔兰曾经遭受英国殖民统治，激起了爱尔兰民众的强烈不满。剧中Mareen曾去英国谋生，饱受歧视，这进一步强化了她对英国的负面情绪。

10. 爱尔兰的乡村生活封闭狭隘，电影是在乡村生活的人们了解世界的一个窗口。这里，Mareen在想象她和Pato告别的场景，如同电影画面一般。
11. **Complan:** 康普伦，用于补充营养的速溶饮品品牌。剧中Mareen常冲调结块的康普伦给母亲Mag喝，以示对母亲的不满。
12. **Rory's:** 酒店名。
13. 这句话表现了Ray对神父的反感。绝大部分爱尔兰人信奉天主教，但教会接二连三发生的丑闻逐渐引起民众的不满。
14. **Australian oul shite:** 澳洲的肥皂剧。
15. **Kimberleys:** 金佰利饼干。剧中Mareen说自己讨厌金佰利饼干，只是买来折磨她妈妈的。
16. **Wagon Wheels:** 马车轮饼干。
17. Mareen和Pato第一次约会时，Pato亲昵地称她为“丽南镇的美人”，并在她房里过夜。

四、拓展思考

1. Do you think Pato sent letters to Maureen or not? Who is lying in the play? Who turns to be more reliable?
2. How do you think of the mother-daughter relationship between Maureen and Mag? What are the main factors to be traced in the selected scenes to this unconventional relationship?
3. Scene Ⅷ is very short. How do you understand its function between scene Ⅶ and scene Ⅸ? Is it a soliloquy in terms of form?
4. Why is the play entitled as *The Beauty Queen of Leenane*? How do you interpret the connotation of queen in the play?

五、延展阅读

麦克多纳在1996年创作的《丽南镇的美人》已经成为当今爱尔兰戏剧舞台的一部当代经典了。从1996—2015年的近20年里，该剧不断上演，成为麦克多纳戏剧中最具知名度的

一部。本章选摘的最后三幕也是全剧的高潮。剧中所描述的女儿用热油浇淋母亲的情景，让读者心惊胆战。这种场面同样在舞台上得以淋漓地体现，带给观众视觉和听觉上的冲击。这种戏剧形式是20世纪90年代以英国新锐剧作家萨拉·凯恩（Sarah Kane，1971—）为代表的戏剧家在戏剧舞台上的探索——直面戏剧（In-yer-face Theatre）。“直面戏剧”通过在舞台上展现暴力和恐怖，在带给观众最具冲击力的直观感受的同时也希望暨此在艺术形式的深层次上进一步探索亚里士多德所强调的戏剧产生恐惧和怜悯的功能。

“直面戏剧”这个概念首先是由英国著名的戏剧评论家希尔兹（Aleks Sierz）提出的，首次出现在他的专著《直面戏剧：英国戏剧的今天》（*In-Yer-Face Theatre: British Drama Today*）里。“直面戏剧”概括了90年代英国新戏剧和舞台艺术的新特色。

“直面”一词最早出现在1976年美国的一个体育新闻报道里。80年代以后，该词逐渐进入主流的英语俚语体系里，但其拼法也曾一度有所改变，如媒体上的“in yo face”，英国乐队命名的“In Yer Face”，《牛津英语字典》则更倾向于带连字符的形容词形式“in-yer-face”。

对于“直面”一词，不同的英语字典有不同的强调解析。1998年版《牛津英语字典》将其定义为“极端具有侵略性和煽动性，无法忽视或回避”；1998年版《柯斯林英语字典》对“In Yer-Face Theater”的定义增加了“面对面对抗”（confrontational）；2000年版的《美国传统英语语言字典》则将本词解释为“具有大胆、挑衅或冒犯特征的”。它体现着“攻击性、挑衅性和鲁莽性”，代表对常规界限的跨越”。希尔兹在集合了多种释义后，将该词解释为“意味着你正在被驱使着看一个逼近的东西，你的私人空间被侵犯了。它意味着对常规界限的跨越”。词义本身强调的不是编导和观众主观上的“直面”残酷，而是新残酷主义的那种不由分说、朝观众劈头盖脸而来的强烈的感受。简而言之，它是一种能够清晰的把观众放在正在发生的情境内的戏剧；它似乎是充满激情地抓住观众的肩膀剧烈地摇晃，正如地震发生时一样，由不得你逃避，直至得到它想要的反应。

在戏剧界最早使用“直面”一词的不是希尔兹，而是剧作家西蒙·格雷（Simon Gray）。该词出现在格雷2001年2月在伦敦首演的戏剧《捷普斯》（*Japes*）中。剧中的中年作家迈克（Michael Cartts）对一种新的写作方式极为愤怒，将之斥责为“径直冲击”。同年稍后，希尔兹的专著出版。他采用《牛津英文字典》的拼写形式，为专著命名。当然，对于文学现象的命名和归纳总是滞后于现象本身的。

附录 1 常用戏剧术语 [1]

Absurd: a term derived from the existentialism of Albert Camus, and often applied to the modern sense of human purposelessness in a universe without meaning or value. Many 20th century writers of prose fiction have stressed the absurd nature of human existence—notable instances are the novels and stories of Franz Kafka, in which the characters face alarmingly incomprehensible predicaments.

Act: a major division in the action of a play, comprising one or more scenes. A break between acts often coincides with a point at which the plot jumps ahead in time.

Aestheticism: the doctrine or disposition that regards beauty as an end in itself, and attempts to preserve the art forms subordination to moral, didactic, or political purposes. The term is often used synonymously with the Aesthetic Movement, a literary and artistic tendency of the late 19th century which may be understood as a further phase of Romanticism in reaction against philistine bourgeois values of practical efficiency and morality. Aestheticism found theoretical support in the aesthetics of Immanuel Kant and other German philosophers who separated the sense of beauty from practical interests. Elaborated by Théophile Gautier in 1835 as a principle of artistic independence, aestheticism was adopted in France by Baudelaire, Flaubert, and the Symbolists, and in England by Walter Pater, Oscar Wilde, and several poets of the 1890s, under the slogan *l' art pour l' art* ("art for art's sake"). Wilde and other devotees of pure beauty—like the artists Whistler and Beardsley—were sometimes known as aesthetes.

Antagonist: the principal character in opposition to the protagonist or hero or heroine of a narrative or drama. The antagonist is often a villain seeking to frustrate a heroine or hero; but in those works in which the protagonist is represented as evil, the antagonist will often be a virtuous or sympathetic character, as Macduff is in *Macbeth*.

1 本文摘自：波尔蒂克 . 牛津文学术语词典 . 上海：上海外语教育出版社，2000.

Apollonian and Dionysian: terms for the twin principles which the German philosopher Friedrich Nietzsche detected in Greek civilization in his early work *Die Geburt der Tragödie* (*The Birth of Tragedy*, 1872). Nietzsche was challenging the usual view of Greek culture as ordered and serene, emphasizing instead the irrational element of frenzy found in the rites of Dionysus (the god of intoxication known to the Romans as Bacchus). He associated the Apollonian tendency with the instinct for form, beauty, moderation, and symmetry, best expressed in Greek sculpture, while the Dionysian (or Dionysiac) instinct was one of irrationality, violence, and exuberance, found in music. This opposition has some resemblance to that between Classicism and Romanticism. In Nietzsche's theory of drama, the Apollonian (in dialogue) and the Dionysian (in choric song) are combined in early Greek tragedy, but then split apart in the work of Euripides: he hoped at first that Wagner's operas would reunite them.

Arcadia or Arcady: an isolated mountainous region of Greece in the central Peloponnese, famed in the ancient world for its sheep and as the home of the god Pan. It was imagined by Virgil in his *Eclogues* (42-37BC), and by later writers of pastorals in the Renaissance, as an ideal world of rural simplicity and tranquility. The adjective Arcadian can be applied to any such imagined pastoral setting.

Archetype: a symbol, theme, setting, or character-type that recurs in different times and places in myth, literature, folklore, dreams, and rituals so frequently or prominently as to suggest (to certain speculative psychologists and critics) that it embodies some essential element of universal human experience. Examples offered by the advocates of myth criticism include such recurrent symbols as the rose, the serpent, and the sun; common themes like love, death, and conflict; mythical settings like the paradisal garden; stock characters like the femme fatale, the hero, and the magician; and some basic patterns of action and plot such as the quest, the descent to the underworld, or the feud. The most fundamental of these patterns is often said to be that of death and rebirth, reflecting the natural cycle of the seasons: the Canadian critic Northrop Frye put forward an influential model of literature based on this proposition in *Anatomy of Criticism* (1957). Archetypal criticism originated in the early 20th century from the speculations of the British anthropologist J. G. Frazer in the Golden Bough (1890-1915)—a comparative study of mythologies—and from those of the Swiss psychologist C. G. Jung, who in the 1920s proposed that certain symbols in dreams and myths were residues of ancestral memory preserved in the reductionism involved in the application of such unverified hypotheses to literary works and more alert to the cultural differences that the archetypal approach often overlooks in its search for universals.

Art for Art's Sake: the slogan of Aestheticism in the 19th century, often given in its French form as l' art pour l' art. The most important early manifesto for the idea, Theophile Gautier's preface to his novel *Mademoiselle de Maupin* (1835), does not actually use the phrase itself, which is a simplified expression of the principle adopted by many leading French authors and by Walter Pater, Oscar Wilde, and Arthur Symons in England.

Black Comedy: a kind of drama (or, by extension, a non-dramatic work) in which disturbing or sinister subjects like death, disease, or warfare, are treated with bitter amusement, usually in a manner calculated to offend and shock. Prominent in the theater of the absurd, black comedy is also a feature of Joe Orton's *Loot* (1965). A similar black humor is strongly evident in modern American fiction from Nathanael West's *A Cool Million* (1934) to Joseph Heller's *Catch-22* (1961) and Kurt Vonnegut's *Slaughterhouse-Five* (1969).

Brechtian: belonging to or derived from the work of Bertolt Brecht (1989-1956), German poet, playwright, and dramatic theorist. When applied to the work of other dramatists, the term usually indicates their use of the techniques of Epic Theatre, especially the disruption of realistic illusion known as the Alienation Effect.

Carnivalization: the liberating and subversive influence of popular humor on the literary tradition, according to the theory propounded by the Russian linguist Mikhail Bakhtin in his works *Problems of Dostoevsky's Poetics* (1929) and *Rabelais and his World* (1965). Bakhtin argued that the overturning of hierarchies in popular carnival—its mingling of the sacred with the profane, the sublime with the ridiculous—lies behind the most open (Dialogic or Polyphonic) literary genres, notably Menippean satire and the novel, especially since the Renaissance. Carnivalized literary forms allow alternative voices to dethrone the authority of official culture: Rabelais, for example, subverts the asceticism of the medieval Church by giving free rein to the bodily profanity of folk festivities.

Celtic Revival: a term sometimes applied to the period of Irish literature in English (c.1885-1939) now more often referred to as the Irish literary Revival or Renaissance. There are other similar terms: Celtic Renaissance, Celtic Dawn, and Celtic Twilight (the last famously mocked by James Joyce as the 'cultic twalette'). These Celtic titles are misleading as descriptions of the broader Irish Revival, but they indicate a significant factor in the early phase of the movements: Celticism involves an idea of Irishness based on fanciful notions of innate racial character outlined by the English critic Matthew Arnold in *On the Study of Celtic Literature* (1866), in which Celtic traits are said to include delicacy, charm, spirituality, and ineffectual sentimentality. This image of Irishness was adopted in part by W. B. Yeats in his attempt to create a distinctively Irish literature with his dreamy early verse and with *The Celtic Twilight* (1893), a collection of stories based on Irish folklore and fairy-tales. Apart from the poet 'AE' (George Russell), the other major figures in the Irish Literary Revival—Synge. O'Casey, and Joyce—had little or nothing to do with such Celticism.

Character: character is another important aspect of drama. Aristotle places it immediately after plot for in his analysis plot is character in action. Similar to other literary forms such as fiction and novel, character in drama can be portrayed in three ways. First, character is described by appearance. Actors' physical appearance can usually give audiences a direct and immediate impression of what kind of person the character is. Second, character is revealed by speech. Third, character is established by action. A character's external actions give readers clues to his or her emotions. Sometimes, the playwright may create a misleading or ambiguous impression of a character at the beginning of the play and then gradually reveal the truth as the play progresses. Sometimes, the playwright will deliberately leave audiences in a state of confusion of what kind of person the character is. But the more usual practice of most dramatists is to dispose the genuine nature and background of character through the speech of others.

Chorus: a group of singers distinct from the principal performers in a dramatic or musical performance; also the song or refrain that they sing. In Classical Greek Tragedy a chorus of twelve or fifteen masked performers would sing, with dancing movements, a commentary on the action of the play, interpreting its events from the standpoint of traditional wisdom. This practice appears to have been derived from the choral lyrics of religious festival. The Greek tradition of choral lyric includes the dithyramb, the paean, and the choral odes of

Pindar. In some Elizabethan plays, like Shakespeare's *Henry V*, a single character called a chorus introduces the setting and action. Except in opera, the group chorus is used rarely in modern European drama: examples are T. S. Eliot's *Murder in the Cathedral* (1935) and Brecht's *The Caucasian Chalk Circle* (1948). The term has also been applied to certain groups of characters in novels, who view the main action from the standpoint of rural tradition, as in some works of George Eliot, Thomas Hardy, and William Faulkner.

Chronicle Play: a history play, especially of the kind written in England in the 1950s and based upon the revised 1587 edition of Raphael Holinshed's *Chronicles*. This group of plays includes Marlowe' s *Edward II* (1592) and the three parts of Shakespeare's *Henry VI* (c.1590-2).

Comedy: in the most common literary application, a comedy is a fictional work in which the materials are selected and managed primarily in order to interest and amuse us. The characters and their discomfitures engage our pleasurable attention rather than our profound concern. We are made to feel confident that no great disaster will occur, and usually the action turns out happily for the chief characters.

Defamiliarization: the distinctive effect achieved by literary works in disrupting our habitual perception of the world, enabling us to "see" things afresh, according to the theories of some English Romantic poets and of Russian Formalism, Samuel Taylor Coleridge in *Biographia Literaria* (1817) wrote of the "film of familiarity" that blinds us to the wonders of the world, and that Wordworth's poetry aimed to remove. P. B. Shelly in his essay *The Defense of Poetry* (written 1821) also claims that poetry "makes familiar objects be as if they were not familiar" by stripping "the veil of familiarity from the world". In modern usage, the term corresponds to Viktor Shklovsky's use of the Russian word *ostranenie* ("making strange") in his influential essay *Poetry as Technique* (1917). Shklovsky argued that art exists in order to recover for us the sensation of life which is diminished in the "automatized" routine of everyday experience. He and the other Formalists set out to define the devices by which literary works achieve this effect, usually in terms of the "foregrounding" of the linguistic medium. Brecht's theory of the alienation effect in drama starts from similar grounds.

Diction: diction refers to the language of the play, the words which the actors speak. Dramatists usually have utilitarian requirements for the discourse they employ in a play. First, the dialogue must be simple, concise and interesting, for the words must be immediately understood by audiences; second, it should capture the spirit of time. For example, the diction in Shakespeare's plays represent the trend of history at that period; third, it must be appropriate both for the character and the situation; forth, it should be dynamic enough to reveal the characters' relationship to each other, to indicate what is happening inside the character and thus to reflect the progression of the action; finally, good dramatic language must be suited for oral speaking, for in the theater, there is no turning back the page and no pause to weigh and consider a line before continuing to the next.

Drama: the form of composition designed for performance in the theater, in which actors take the roles of the characters, perform the indicated action, and utter the written dialogue. (The common alternative name for a dramatic composition is a play.) In poetic drama the dialogue is written in verse, which in English is usually bland verse. Almost all the heroic dramas of the English Restoration Period, however, were written in heroic couplets (iambic pentameter lines rhyming in pairs). A closet drama is written in dramatic form, with dialogue, indicated settings, and stage directions, but is intended by the author to be read rather than to be performed.

Expressionism: a general term for a mode of literary or visual art which, in extreme reaction against Realism or Naturalism, presents a world violently distorted under the pressure of intense personal moods, ideas, and emotions: image and language thus express feeling and imagination rather than represent external reality. Although not an organized movement, expressionism was an important factor in the painting, drama, poetry, and cinema of German-speaking Europe between 1910 and 1924. The term did not come into use until 1911, but has since been applied retrospectively to some important forerunners of expressionist technique, going as far back as Georg Büchner's plays of the 1830s and Vincent Van Gogh's paintings of the 1880s; other significant precursors include the Norwegian painter Edvard Munch, the Swedish playwright August Strindberg (in his *Dream Play*, 1902), and the German playwright Frank Wedekind. Within the period 1910-1924, consciously expressionist techniques of abstraction were promoted by Wassily Kandinsky and the "Blue Rider" group of painter, while in drama various anti-naturalist principles of abstract characterization and structural discontinuity were employed in the plays of Ernst Toller, Georg Kaiser, and Walter Hasenclever; these had some influence on the early plays of Bertolt Vrecht, notably *Baal* (1922). The poetry of Georg Trakl, Gottfried Benn, August Stramm, and Franz Werfel displayed comparable distortions of accepted structures and syntax in favous of symbolized mood. The nightmarish labyrinths of Franz Kafka's novels are the nearest equivalent in prose fiction. German expressionism is best known today through the wide influence of its cinematic masterpiece: Robert Wiene's *The Cabinet of Dr Caligari* (1920), F. W. Murnau's *Nosferatu* (1922), and Fritz Lang's *Metropolis* (1926). Along with their much-imitated visual patterns of sinister shadows, these films reveal a shared obsession with automatized, trance-like states, which appears in expressionist literature too: a common concern of expressionism is with the eruption of irrational and chaotic forces from beneath the surface of a mechanized modern world. Some of its explosive energies issued into Data, Vorticism, and other Avant-Garde movements of the 1920s. In the English-speaking world, expressionist dramatic techniques were adopted in some of the plays of Eugene O'Neill and Sean O'Casey, and in the "Circe" episode of James Joyce's novel *Ulysses* (1922); in poetry, T. S. Eliot *The Waste Land* (1922) may be considered expressionist in its fragmentary rendering of post-war desolation. In a further sense, the term is sometimes applied to the belief that literary works are essentially expressions of their authors' moods and thoughts; this has been dominant assumption about literature since the rise of Romanticism.

History Play: a play representing events drawn wholly or partly from recorded history. The term usually refers to Chronicle Plays, especially those of Shakespeare, but it also covers some later works such as Schiller's *Maria Stuart* (1800) and John Osborne's *Luther* (1961). In a somewhat looser sense, it has been applied also to some plays that take as their subject the impact of historical change on the lives of fictional characters: David Hare's *Licking Hitler* (1978) has been reprinted with two other works under the title *The History Plays* (1984).

Masque or Mask: a spectacular kind of indoor performance combining poetic drama, music, dance, song, lavish costume, and costly stage effects, which was favored by European royalty in the 16th and early 17th centuries. Members of the court would enter disguised, taking the parts of mythological persons, and enact a simple allegorical plot, concluding with the removal of masks and a dance joined by members of the audience. Shakespeare included a short masque scene in *The Tempest* (1611), and Milton's play *Comus*

(1634) is loosely related to the masque; these are now the best-known examples, but at the courts of James I and Charles I the highest form of the masque proper was represented by the quarrelsome collaboration of Ben Jonson with the designer Inigo Jones from 1605 to 1631 in the hugely expensive *Oberon* (1611) and other works. The parliamentary Revolution of the 1640s brought this form of extravagance to an abrupt end.

Melodrama: the term melodrama refers to a dramatic work that puts characters in a lot of danger in order to appeal to the emotions. It may also refer to the genre which includes such works, or to language, behavior, or events which resemble them. It is based around having the same character in every scene, often a hero, damsel in distress, a villain. It is also used in scholarly and historical musical contexts to refer to dramas of the 18th and 19th centuries in which orchestral music or song was used to accompany the action.

Metadrama or Metatheatre: drama about drama, or any moment of self-consciousness by which a play draws attention to its own fictional status as a theatrical pretence. Normally, direct addresses to the audience in prologues, epilogues, and inductions are metadramatic in that they refer to the play itself and acknowledge the theatrical situation; a similar effect may be achieved in asides. In a more extended sense, the use of a play-within-the-play, as in *Hamlet*, allows a further metadramatic exploration of the nature of theater, which is taken still further in plays about plays, such as Luigi Pirandello's *Sei personaggi in cerca d'autore* (*Six Characters in Search of an Author*, 1921).

Miracle Play: a kind of medieval religious play representing non-scriptural legends of saints or of the Virgin Mary. The term is often confusingly applied also to the Mystery Plays, which form a distinct body of drama based on biblical stories. Thanks to the book-burning zeal of the English Reformation, no significant miracle plays survive in English, but there is a French cycle of forty *Miracles de Notre-Dame* probably dating from the 14th century.

Monodrama: a play or dramatic scene in which only one character speaks; or a sequence of dramatic monologues all spoken by the same single character. The second sense is rarely used, except of Tennyson's *Maud* (1855), to which the author attached the subtitle *A Monodrama* in 1875. In the first sense, some German playwrights of the late 18th century wrote monodramas that had musical accompaniment, notably J. C. Brandes's *Ariadne auf Naxos* (1774). Modern writers of monodramas include Samuel Beckett in *Krapp's Last Tape* (1958) and Alan Bennett, who has written several monodramas for television. See also Monologue.

Monologue: an extended speech uttered by one speaker, either to others or as if alone. Significant varieties include the Dramatic Monologue (a kind of poem in which the speaker is imagined to be addressing a silent audience), and the Soliloquy (in which the speaker is supposed to be "overheard" while alone). Some modern plays in which only one character speaks, like Beckett's *Krapp's Last Tape* (1958), are known either as monodramas or as monologues. In prose fiction, the interior monologue is a representation of a character's unspoken thoughts, sometimes rendered in the style known as Stream of Consciousness. The speaker of a monologue is sometimes called monologuist.

Morality Play: a kind of religious drama popular in England, Scotland, France, and elsewhere in Europe in the 15th and early 16th centuries. Morality plays are dramatized allegories, in which personified virtues, vices, diseases, and temptations struggle for the soul of Man as he travels from birth to death. They instill a simple message of Christian salvation, but often include comic scenes, as in the lively *obscenities of Mankind* (c.1465). The earliest surviving example in English is the long *Castle of Perseverance* (c.1420), and the best-known is *Everyman* (c.1510). Most are anonymous, but *Magnyfycence* (c. 1515) was written by John Skelton. Echoes of the morality plays can be found in Elizabethan drama, especially Marlowe's *Dr Faustus* and the character of Iago in Shakespeare's *Othello*, who resembles the sinister tempter know as the Vice in morality plays.

Music: refers to all of the auditory aspect of a play, including sound effects and the tonal pattern of the spoken word. Many great playwrights are expert in making use of the sound to enhance the effect of a play. For instance, in Eugene O'Neill's *The Emperor Jones*, the sound of the African drama throughout the play not only intensifies the sense of fear but also assumes the role of an invisible force throughout the play.

Naturalism: a more deliberate kind of realism in novels, stories and plays, usually involving a view of human beings as passive victims of natural forces and social environment. As a literary movement, naturalism was initiated in France by Jules and Edmond Goncourt with their novel *Germinie Lacerteux* (1865), but it came to be led by Emile Zola, who claimed a "scientific" status for his studies of impoverished characters miserably subjected to hunger, sexual obsession, and hereditary defects in *Thérèse Raquin* (1867), *Germinal* (1885), and many other novels. Naturalist fiction aspired to a sociological objectivity, offering detailed and fully researched investigations into unexplored corners of modern society—railways in Zola's *La Bête humaine* (1890), the department store in his *Au Bonheur des dames* (1883)—while enlivening this with a new sexual sensationalism. Other novelists and storytellers associated with naturalism include Alphonse Daudet and Guy de Maupassant in France, Theodore Dreiser and Frank Norris in the United States, and George Moore and George Gissing in England; the most significant work of naturalism in English being Dreiser's *Sister Carrie* (1990). In the theatre, Henrik Ibsen's play *Ghosts* (1881), with its stress on heredity, encouraged an important tradition of dramatic naturalism led by August Strindberg, Gerhart Hauptmann, and Maxim Gorky; in a somewhat looser sense, the realistic plays of Anton Chekhov are sometimes grouped with the naturalist phase of European drama at the turn of the century. The term Naturalistic in drama usually has a broader application, denoting a very detailed illusion of real life on the stage, especially in speech, costume, and sets.

Parody: a mocking imitation of the style of a literary work or works, ridiculing the stylistic habits of an author or school by exaggerated mimicry. Parody is related to burlesque in its application of serious styles to ridiculous subjects, to satire in its punishment of eccentricities, and even to criticism in its analysis of style. The Greek dramatist Aristophanes parodied the styles of Aeschylus and Euripides in *The Frogs* (405BC), while Cervantes parodied chivalric romances in *Don Quixote* (1605). In English, two of the leading parodists are Henry Fielding and James Joyce. Poets in the 19th century, especially William Wordsworth and Robert Browning, suffered numerous parodies of their works.

Plot: Aristotle places plot foremost in his list of ingredients that composes drama, for it provides the basic framework of the action. "Plot" is basically another term for structure; the things that happen in the play and the ways in which those incidents connects. Traditionally, a typical dramatic plot consists of five parts: (1) the exposition, i.e., the exposing of facts, the presentation and definition of the established situation from which the play takes rise; (2) the rising action, in which the plottings and counter-plottings, accumulation of incidents and development of characters complicate the original situation; (3) the climax or rising point, which reverses the emotional tone and direction of the action and after which nothing new can be added; (4) the falling action, in which the various complications begin to find their resolution; and (5) the conclusion or denouement, which establishes a new situation to end the play.

Poetic Drama: the category of plays written wholly or mainly in verse. This includes most tragedies and other serious plays from the earliest times to the 19th century, along with most comedy up to the late 17th century. Strictly speaking, the term is not identical with dramatic poetry, which also includes verse compositions not suited for the stage, such as Closet Dramas.

Problem Play: usually a play dealing with a particular social problem in a realistic manner designed to change public opinion; also called a thesis play. Significant examples are Henrik Ibsen's *A Doll's House* (1879), on women's subordination in marriage, and George Bernard Shaw's *Mrs. Warren's Profession* (1902) on prostitution. In studies of Shakespeare, however, the term has been used to designate a group of his plays written in the first years of the 17th century: the dark comedies *Measure for Measure* and *All's Well That Ends Well*, and the tragicomedy *Troilus and Cressida*. Critics have often been distributed by the somber and cynical mood of these plays, which seems to clash oddly with their comic conventions.

Protagonist: the main character in a drama or other literary work, who may also be opposed by an Antagonist. Originally, in ancient Greek theatre, the protagonist was the principal actor in a drama.

Realism: a mode of writing that gives the impression of recording or "reflecting" faithfully an actual way of life. The term refers, sometimes confusingly, both to a literary method based on detailed accuracy of description (i.e. Verisimilitude) and to a more general attitude that rejects idealization, escapism, and other extravagant qualities of romance in favor of recognizing soberly the actual problems of life. Modern criticism frequently insists that realism is not a direct or simple reproduction of reality (a "slice of life") but a system of conventions producing a lifelike illusion of some "real" world outside the text, by processes of selection, exclusion, description, and manners of addressing the reader. In its methods and attitudes, realism may be found as an element in many kinds of writing prior to the 19th century (e.g. in Chaucer or Defoe, in their different ways); but as a dominant literary trend it is associated chiefly with the 19th century novel of middle-or lower-class life, in which the problems of ordinary people in unremarkable circumstances are rendered with close attention to the details of physical setting and to the complexities of social life. The outstanding works of realism in 19th century fiction include Honoré de Balzac's *Illusions perdus* (1837-1843), Gustave Flaubert's *Madame Bovary* (1857), and George Eliot's *Middlemarch* (1871-1872). In France, a self-consciously realist school announced itself in 1857 with the publication of Champfleury's *Le Réalisme*, but the term normally refers to the general convention rather than to this barely significant group. In the work of some novelists, realism passes over into the movement of naturalism, in which sociological investigation and determinist views of human behaviour predominate. Realism also established itself as an important tradition in the theater in the late of 19th and early 20th centuries, in the work of Henrik Ibsen, George Bernard Shaw, and others; and it remains a standard convention of film and television drama. Despite the radical attempts of modernism to displace the realist emphasis on external reality (notably in the movements of expressionism and surrealism), realism survived as a major current within 20th century fiction, sometimes under the label of neo-realism.

Revenge Tragedy: a kind of tragedy popular in England from 1590s to the 1630s, following the success of Thomas Kyd's sensational play *The Spanish Tragedy* (c.1589). Its action is typically centered upon a leading character's attempt to avenge the murder of a loved one, sometimes at the prompting of the victim's ghost; it involves complex intrigues and disguises, and usually some exploration of the morality of revenge. Drawing partly on precedents in Senecan Tragedy, the English revenge tragedy is far more bloodthirsty in its explicit presentation of premeditated violence, and so the more gruesome examples such as Shakespeare's *Titus Andronicus* are sometimes called 'tragedies of blood'. Notable examples of plays that are fully or partly within the revenge tradition are Christopher Marlowe's *The Jew of Malta*, Cyril Tourneur's *The Revenger's Tragedy*, John Webster's *The Duchess of Malfi*, and John Ford's *'Tis Pity She's a Whore*. A more famous play drawing on the revenge conventions is Shakespeare's *Hamlet*.

Scene: in a drama, a subdivision of an act or of a play not divided into acts. A scene normally represents actions happening in one place at one time, and is marked off from the next scene by a curtain, a blackout, or a brief emptying of the stage. In the study of narrative works, "scene" is also the name given to a "dramatic" method of narration that presents events at roughly the same pace as that at which they are supposed to be occurring, i.e. usually in detail and with substantial use of dialogue. In this sense the scenic narrative method is contrasted with summary, in which the duration of the story's events is compressed into a brief account.

Self-reflexive: a term applied to literary works that openly reflect upon their own processes of artful composition. Such self-referentiality is frequently found in modern works of fiction that repeatedly refer to their own fictional status. The narrator in such works, and in their earlier equivalents such as Sterne's *Tristram Shandy* (1759-1767), is sometimes called a "self-conscious narrator". Self-reflexivity may also be found in poetry.

Spectacle: spectacle concerns all of the visual aspects of a play: the scenery, light effect, blocking, costume, make-up, etc. They make drama on stage quite impressive to audiences. For example, in Act I, Scene II of *Hamlet*, when the Queen asks Hamlet to "cast thy nighted color off," Hamlet should obviously be dressed in black. Hamlet dressed in black in this scene is a typical example of how a playwright can invent a striking stage effect through character's costume. Hamlet enters at the beginning of the scene with the king, the Queen, and the courtiers, who all dress in gaudery. However, he is dressed in black, which shows that he is silent and isolated from the other figures. The stage picture has an effect which is very striking in performance.

Subplot: a secondary sequence of actions in a dramatic or narrative work, usually involving characters of lesser importance (and often of lower social status). The subplot may be related to the main plot as a parallel or contrast, or it may be more or less separate from it. Subplots are especially common in Elizabethan and Jacobean drama, a famous example being that of Gloucester and his sons in Shakespeare's *King Lear*; but they are also found in long novels such as those of Dickens.

Symbolism: refers to the use of symbols, or to a set of related symbols; however, it is also the name given to an important movement in late 19th century and early 20th century poetry: for this sense, see Symbolists. One of the important features of Romanticism and succeeding phases of Western literature was a much more pronounced reliance upon enigmatic symbolism in both poetry and prose fiction, sometimes involving obscure private codes of meaning, as in the poetry of *Blake or Yeats*. A well-known early example of this is the albatross in Coleridge's *The Rime of the Ancient Mariner* (1798). Many novelists—notably Herman Melville and D. H. Lawrence—have used symbolic methods; in Melville's *Moby-Dick* (1851) the White Whale (and indeed almost every object and character in the book) becomes a focus for many different suggested meanings. Melville's extravagant symbolism was encouraged partly by the importance which American Transcendentalism gave to symbolic interpretation of the world.

Theatre of the Absurd: the critic Martin Esslin coined the phrase in 1961 to refer to a number of dramatists of the 1950s (led by Samuel Beckett and Eugene Ionesco) whose works evoke the absurd by abandoning logical form, character, and dialogue together with realistic illusion. The classic work of absurdist theatre is Beckett's *En attendant Godot* (*Waiting for Godot*, 1952), which revives some of the conventions of clowning and farce to represent the impossibility of purposeful action and the paralysis of human aspiration. Other dramatists associated with the theatre of the absurd include Edward Albee, Jean Genet, Harold Pinter, and Vaclav Havel.

Thought: Thought in drama may include the following two layers of meanings. First, it refers to the rationale of individual characters in a play. Characters in drama will make subjective decisions or will be caught in conflicting emotional entanglement, which will all be reflected as their thought. Second, thought also concerns a play's theme which summarizes the moral and indicates the symbolic meaning of the play as a whole.

Tragedy: the term is broadly applied to literary, and especially to dramatic, representations of serious actions which eventuate in a disastrous conclusion for the protagonist (the chief character).

Tragicomedy: a type of Elizabethan and Jacobean drama which intermingled both the standard characters and subject matter and the standard plot-forms of tragedy and comedy. Tragicomedy represented a serious action which threatened a tragic disaster to the protagonist, yet, by an abrupt reversal of circumstance, turned out happily.

Well-made Play: now a rather unfavorable term for a play that is neatly efficient in the construction of its plot but superficial in ideas and characterization. In 19th century France, the term (pièce bien faite) at first had a more positive sense, denoting the carefully constructed suspense in comedies and melodramas by Eugène Scribe (1791—1861) and his follower Victorien Sardou (1831-1908). As this tradition was displaced by the more serious concerns of dramatic naturalism, the term acquired its dismissive sense, especially in the critical writings of G. B. Shaw.

附录 2　走近爱尔兰：爱尔兰历史简述[1]

爱尔兰地处欧洲，西濒大西洋，东临爱尔兰海，与英国隔海相望。因四面环海，其漫长的海岸和绵延的山峦峭壁构成爱尔兰独特而宝贵的旅游资源。爱尔兰属于温带海洋性气候，常年气候温和、多雨湿润。其绿地覆盖面大，耕地和林地占总面积的75%，因此，爱尔兰又素有“绿翡翠”之称。

对于很多人而言，“爱尔兰”与“爱尔兰岛”、“爱尔兰共和国”（Republic of Ireland）、“北爱尔兰”（Northern Ireland）常被混为一谈，无法分辨。事实上，8.4万平方公里、包含32个郡的爱尔兰岛被割裂为两个部分：南方的爱尔兰共和国和北方的北爱尔兰。南方的爱尔兰共和国是拥有独立主权的政体，而由北方6郡组成的北爱尔兰仅仅是一个行政区域，与苏格兰、威尔士和英格兰共同构成“大不列颠及北爱尔兰联合王国”（Great Britain and Northern Ireland）。1921年才正式使用的北爱尔兰，虽然其官方英文称谓是Northern Ireland（北爱尔兰），但很多爱尔兰人仍称之为North of Ireland（爱尔兰北方）。显然，爱尔兰岛今日割裂的状态源于爱尔兰与英国悠远而“纠缠”的历史关系。

除上述4个带有“爱尔兰”关键词的名称外，还有一个经常在爱尔兰文学作品中出现的词——“阿尔斯特”（Ulster）。“阿尔斯特”一词是随着“北爱尔兰”的显现确立后在政治话语中变成隐身的一个概念。历史上，“阿尔斯特”是爱尔兰岛古代区域划分的4个省份之一，也是爱尔兰岛上开发规模最大的一个区域。17世纪初，苏格兰国王詹姆斯四世入主英格兰转身成为斯图亚特王朝的詹姆斯一世时，他力主英格兰和苏格兰贵族来此地域，开发新的种植园（Plantation）。三个世纪的开发使贝尔法斯特和都柏林成为爱尔兰岛上最发达的两个中心点。1921年，历史上包含9个郡的阿尔斯特一分为二，其中6郡并称为北爱尔兰，剩余的3郡归属爱尔兰共和国。

据史料记载，爱尔兰岛最早的居民是凯尔特人（Celts）。他们约在公元前5世纪从奥地利、高卢（现今的法国、比利时和瑞士）跨海而来。这些从欧洲大陆来的凯尔特人给爱尔兰带来了凯尔特语言（Celtic）和凯尔特文化（Celtic paganism）[2]。在古典作家的笔下，凯尔特人往往被描述为身材魁伟、长颅白肌、金发碧眼，是英勇善战的勇士。

熟悉英国历史的读者知道，公元前5世纪到5世纪的英伦本岛正值罗马统治时期（Roman Conquest）。与身形高大的凯尔特人相比，罗马人身材相对矮小、肤色略暗、发

1　本文摘自李成坚的学术专著《当代爱尔兰戏剧研究》之序言的第一小节。

2　凯尔特文化是最早进入爱尔兰的文化。但随着文化分支的不断演进、英国文化的入侵，凯尔特文化中的很多习俗一度被认为是异教文化，排斥在爱尔兰文化范畴之外。

色眼色较深。恺撒曾提到，当年古罗马人远征高卢时，以其身材之相对矮小而颇受高卢人的轻视。可见英国和爱尔兰的历史发端均是来自欧洲大陆的族群。

公元432年，圣帕特里克（St. Patrick）——一位基督教罗马官员的儿子，将基督教传入爱尔兰。相传，帕特里克是被发送到爱尔兰岛牧羊的俘虏。他在六年的牧羊岁月中，不忘他的宗教使命，坚持传播基督教。公元5世纪，爱尔兰被基督教化，相较于公元7世纪才进入基督教化时代的英国早了近两个世纪。爱尔兰共和国的国庆日3月17日是帕特里克的生日，故国庆日又称圣帕特里克日（St. Patrick Day）。

公元8世纪末，强悍的北欧海盗—维京人（Vikings），从斯堪的纳维亚半岛出发，同时登陆英伦岛和爱尔兰岛。两个地区均进入维京统治时代。尽管维京人的时代在公元11世纪结束，但今天的爱尔兰诸多城市，如都柏林、科克（Cork）和利姆瑞克（Limerick）等市区仍可见维京人在建筑、艺术品制作等方面留下的古老痕迹。在都柏林的市区旅游项目中，有一个名为“维京之旅”（Viking Tour）的车游活动，即以双层旅游巴士带游客重走当年维京人进入都柏林的路线。这一项目因惊险刺激深受青少年游客的欢迎。

在维京人统治时代的后期，即公元10世纪，爱尔兰岛南部出现了第一个“强大”的本土王朝——博鲁王朝（Boru Dynasty），为爱尔兰留下了考古发现的最早历史和文学文献。尽管11世纪维京人日渐式微，欧洲大陆一支新的强族诺曼人（Norman）崛起，1014年科伦塔夫一役（Battle of Clontarf），博鲁王朝被维京人消灭。至12世纪，爱尔兰岛再没有出现过超越博鲁王朝的王国。岛上诸多小国林立，终年纷争。

1166年，莱茵斯特国王（King of Leinster）麦克穆诺（Dermot MacMurrough）处于四面受敌之际，于是他率部众跨过爱尔兰海，登陆布里斯托，向英王亨利二世（King Henry II of England）求助。1169年，亨利二世军队登上爱尔兰岛，1171年，亨利二世自称爱尔兰领王（Lord of Ireland），正式拉开了英国人在爱尔兰行使统治权力的历史序幕。

一直以来，学术界对于爱尔兰是否应归于后殖民主义理论探讨范畴存在诸多分歧。尽管很多人坚持认为爱尔兰人是英国在欧洲大陆的第一个殖民地，但中世纪很长一段时期，英国也处于“外族”入侵的被动时期。1066年，随着说法语的诺曼人入主英伦岛，英国也进入了它的第3个“外族”统治时期——诺曼统治时期（Norman Conquest）。从11世纪到15世纪，即英国第一个真正的王朝“多铎王朝”（Tudor Dynasty）建立之期，英国在其封建社会形态之时，经历了不同族群的融合（盎格鲁—诺曼人）、王朝的整顿（红白玫瑰战争），最重要的是民族意识的萌芽（多铎王朝建立）。一定意义上，封建时代英王在爱尔兰的统治并非现代意义上的殖民统治。此外，亨利二世的后继统治者们，如理查二世、理查四世、亨利七世等在爱尔兰推行英国的政令，试图使爱尔兰和英国同质化的努力似乎并不见效，相反，盎格鲁—诺曼人在爱尔兰的佩尔地区（Pale）[3]似乎渐渐融入盖尔人的文化

3 佩尔地区（Pale）是英国人对以都柏林为中心的区域的称谓，专指英国统治者集中居住的地区，佩尔以外是爱尔兰本土人的居住区。

习俗之中，“比盖尔人更盖尔特”[4]，征服者为被征服者征服。英国文艺复兴时代巨擘们的作品中，如莎士比亚的历史剧、斯宾塞的政论文《爱尔兰当前现状》或隐或显地展现了英格兰民族崛起后在爱尔兰“统治”的失败和英格兰中心主义意识作用下的文化焦虑[5]。

然而，自16世纪英国国王亨利八世宣布与罗马天主教廷脱离，创建英国国教——新教（Protestantism）以来，以离婚案为导火索的英国宗教改革本质上是英国资产阶级壮大的内在需求，标志着英国资产阶级势力的强盛、英国民族意识的觉醒。16世纪下半叶，伊丽莎白女王时期，英国的经济、军事力量进一步强大，愈发膨胀的英格兰民族中心主义意识加速了英国在爱尔兰同质化的努力。

16世纪末、17世纪初英国统治者们意识到英人在爱尔兰的“堕落”，自此在爱尔兰开启了武力殖民、加速了文化殖民的步伐。1541年，亨利八世正式在爱尔兰称王（King of Ireland）。1603年，英国与爱尔兰在金赛尔交战（Battle of Kinsale），爱尔兰战败，盖尔领主纷纷逃离爱尔兰岛，盖尔秩序和盖尔文化自此在爱尔兰岛走向失落。17世纪英国资产阶级革命时期（又称清教革命），清教徒克伦威尔率军登上爱尔兰岛。因革命期间，信奉天主教的爱尔兰人支持了最终在革命中失败的詹姆斯二世，因而克伦威尔在爱尔兰岛上对天主教村庄进行大肆杀戮，从此埋下了天主教与新教对立的仇恨种子。

16—17世纪无论是对英国还是爱尔兰，都是关键的历史时期。于英格兰，历经了一系列重大历史事件：宗教改革、文艺复兴的黄金时代、海上霸主地位确立、资产阶级革命、王朝复辟、君主立宪制确定。16—17世纪是英格兰民族强盛后民族意识走向自觉、文化中心主义形成与日渐膨胀的重要时期，同时也是宗教上血雨腥风的宗派斗争的拉锯时期。英格兰天主教与新教之间的宗派斗争从16世纪延续到17世纪，成为这两个世纪英国政治斗争的根源所在。

天主教和新教的宗派冲突并不仅仅局限在英格兰本土，它还蔓延到爱尔兰海另一边的土地，深刻地影响着爱尔兰17世纪以来的历史和文化走向。随着英国在爱尔兰推行国教新教的同时，在爱尔兰的旧式天主教英格兰人渐渐从统治者沦落为被统治者。一方面，他们的生活习性逐步被盖尔文化同化；另一方面，17世纪开启了贝尔法斯特地区的新教种植园开垦运动，贝尔法斯特地区成为英国和苏格兰新教派的集中地，而都柏林则是旧式英格兰天主教徒的活动中心。以都柏林（即佩尔地区）为中心的旧式英格兰人渐渐与土著爱尔兰天主教人合流，共同反抗英格兰新教派，成为资产阶级革命时期保皇派的坚决拥护者，站到了英格兰新教派的对立面，爱尔兰成为失败的英格兰保皇派流亡海外的中转站。因而，英爱之间这一错综复杂的宗教历史文化关联，决定了自17世纪以后的英爱政治关系，更彻底改变了英国在爱尔兰统治（殖民）方式的改变。

---

4 凯尔特（Celt）和盖尔（Gale）的差异在于：欧洲大陆的凯尔特人和凯尔特文化在爱尔兰和苏格兰区域，特称盖尔人和盖尔文化。

5 李成坚．2009.《亨利五世》中麦克莫里斯身份探源．外国文学评论（4）．
李成坚．2011. 斯宾塞眼中的爱尔兰．外国文学评论（2）．

进入18世纪，随着英国最早进入工业革命，英国的强大呈不可阻挡之势，其在爱尔兰武力和文化殖民的统治也愈加不可撼动。1800年，爱尔兰和英国签署条约，成立“不列颠及爱尔兰联合王国”，爱尔兰正式以法律条约的形式被纳入英国的版图。

面对英国自工业革命以后不断强大的势力，几百年来爱尔兰人始终没有放弃争取独立自由的权力。自18世纪以来，涌现了无数反殖民统治的民族解放运动；几个世纪以来，爱尔兰人不断流血失利，但1916年都柏林爆发抗英的“复活节起义”，爱尔兰人终于迎来了独立前的曙光。1921年12月，英爱签署双边条约，允许南方的26郡成立爱尔兰自由邦（Irish Free State），北方6郡改称为北爱尔兰，仍归属英国。1937年，爱尔兰宪法宣布自由邦为共和国。1948年12月，爱尔兰议会通过法律，宣布脱离英联邦。1949年，英国承认爱尔兰共和国独立。爱尔兰共和国退出英联邦，迎来了民族的真正独立。

独立之后的50多年里，爱尔兰创造了骄人的成绩。1973年加入欧盟，爱尔兰经济走向迅速发展，尤其是世纪末的最后10年，政府以宽松的投资环境，吸引大批海外公司投资，大量海外资本涌入，其商业、工业，旅游业，尤其是信息产业迅猛发展，爱尔兰步入“凯尔特虎”经济腾飞时期（Celtic Tiger，1990—2005），人们生活富裕程度达到前所未有的高度。由于其强劲的经济发展能力，爱尔兰成为很多欧洲人梦想的地方，爱尔兰在其历史上首度成为移入国家（Migration），一改爱尔兰人大批移民海外的传统。

2005年后，爱尔兰陷入经济低迷，并与希腊、西班牙、葡萄牙和意大利被戏称为“欧洲五猪国”，成为欧盟经济的“拖累”。可喜的是，2013年下半年，爱尔兰率先摆脱欧债危机援助，以创新型经济成为首个成功脱困国，经济再次走向复苏。

伴随着爱尔兰的政治独立和经济腾飞，20世纪对于爱尔兰民族发展是至关重要的百年。在这百年间，爱尔兰民族意识的觉醒、民族形象的重建、民族身份的叙述、民族性的反思都伴随着爱尔兰步入后殖民时代、北爱尔兰政治危机和全球化经济时代一路走来，文化身份的困惑、焦虑和自觉始终是爱尔兰世纪百年的文化焦点。

与诗歌和小说相比，戏剧作为一种大众化和娱乐化的形式，更广泛地发挥着意识形态的形塑作用。爱尔兰民族戏剧运动在世纪初的爱尔兰文艺复兴运动和民族解放运动中发挥了重要的作用，因而，戏剧为我们考察爱尔兰文学中的精神历程提供了最佳的全景观测点。